CONSCIOUS MEN

Moving Into What Works
Leaving Behind What No Longer Works

JOHN GRAY

ARJUNA ARDAGH

Foreword by Warren Farrell

Press Inquiries to pr@awakespeak.com

Published by Self X Press
An Imprint of Awakening Coaching LLC
420 Nursery St Nevada City CA 95959
consciousmen.com

ISBN: 978-1-890909-22-2

DEDICATION

For the Boys and the Young Men
Coming of Age Today:
You are Our Future
Our Hope
and Our Evolutionary Potential

CONTENTS

FOREWORD

by Warren Farrell, Ph.D.

Conscious Men is precisely what men need at this point in history. Until now, societies survived based on their ability to have their sons be unconscious of their own needs. To survive, we needed boys and men who did not question dying for their country, tribe, or kinship network. We needed them to "buy into" the belief that it would make them a hero, give them glory, and make them loved and respected (even if that meant loved, respected, and dead). To question this would make a man a disappointment to his parents, disrespected by peers, and ineligible for a woman's love.

Now, though, we are experiencing "The Irony of Industrialization." That is, when a society successfully trains its men to focus unconsciously on the ingredients of survival—earning money and becoming a killer-protector—it acquires the luxury of becoming conscious. Ironically, training to be unconscious has created freedom to be conscious.

From "The Irony of Industrialization" emanates the void filled by John Gray and Arjuna Ardagh's *Conscious Men*. Thousands of books have provided men with the guidelines to climbing the ladder of success-as-survival. The need for *Conscious Men* derives from the fact that the handbook for success-as-survival is almost the opposite of the handbook for success as a conscious man.

For example, success as an attorney means learning to argue; being a conscious husband or dad means "listening like the sky." Being a great warrior means developing a "killer reflex"; being a conscious leader and dad means also developing an "empathetic reflex."

Success-as-survival consciousness focused on how to get higher up the ladder faster but not a consciousness as to which wall we wanted to lean the ladder against. It was focused more on profit, and less on pollution, because honor was awarded to the successful CEO more than the environmentally-conscious CEO.

Once a man had children, few dads felt they could afford to be conscious of whether they wanted to be a full-time dad, artist, actor, writer, or contemplator of the path to consciousness. Being a "starving artist" was acceptable for the young single man, or the gay man, but not for what a "real man" became: a dad with children. Until I authored my third reasonably successful book, my own dad couldn't accept that I could be both responsible and an author.

Many of the qualities it took to create a killer-protector consciousness are described by words similar to those in *Conscious Men*. They are words like purpose, mission, loyalty, integrity, and honor.

However, in survival-focused consciousness, purpose and mission were externally defined by parents, religion, the fear of ostracism, and ineligibility for love and respect. In *Conscious Men*, purpose and mission are more internally defined.

Conscious Men guides a man to look within and discover his purpose and mission; to be in touch with his feelings but not ruled by his feelings; to live a life that is in pursuit of his path while honoring the commitments he made during that pursuit.

In the past half-century, the women's movement expanded women's sense of purpose. Now women have options: raise children, raise money, or do some combination of both. This encourages women to be conscious—to look inside of themselves to discover which combination of options suits their personality.

Conscious Men can fill men's "purpose void." It can be the parent, the school, and the mentor for men's roadmap to their discovery of their unique calling.

Conscious Men can also guide the boy or man we love to apply his expanded consciousness to the real world. He will learn new ways of being loyal, new senses of purpose, new forms of humor, new ways of respecting women, and ways to love and be loved not just as a human doing but also as a human being.

Warren Farrell, Ph.D.
Author, *The Myth of Male Power*
Mill Valley, CA. September 11, 2015

INTRODUCTION

Men today all over the world face challenges that no man has faced before in thousands of years.

We only have to go back a couple of generations to find that a man's life was fairly simply defined. He would commonly be educated in an all boys' school. He went through different kinds of rites of passage into manhood, depending on his culture. Then a man would spend his day facing difficult and sometimes dangerous challenges. To the degree that he could be triumphant in those challenges and experience victory, he would feel good about himself and feel he had earned the right to rest and rejuvenation. He would come home to his woman, who most probably spent her day nursing or looking after children, maintaining the home, and preparing and cooking food.

Both genders knew their well-defined roles but eventually felt restrained and constricted by them. It is hard to believe that you only have to go back about a hundred years to a time when most people agreed that women did not have the intelligence to make political choices. They were thought of as "the fairer sex... the weaker sex... who should not 'bother their pretty heads' with the affairs of the world." It was Emmeline Pankhurst, in London, who campaigned for women's right to vote, and the suffragette movement then spread all over the world. By 1920, an unstoppable revolution had begun in the redefining of gender.

Another wave of women's empowerment came in the 1970s, just a few years after the summer of love in 1967. Women claimed their right to participate in all kinds of jobs that had traditionally been reserved for men: lawyer, politician, doctor, minister, business leader. Men grew their hair long, learned to play the guitar, "go with the flow," and "follow your bliss." But women were still campaigning to participate in a world where the rules had been created by men. They were often learning to compete in environments that were running on testosterone. And so, in another wave of liberation in the early part of 21st century, women have started to redefine some of these areas, so the rules are no longer completely set by men. We have seen the emergence of courses in universities on feminine leadership, feminine ecology, and feminine spirituality.

During the last hundred years, as this redefining of gender roles has been primarily initiated by women, men have fallen into a variety of different responses, all of which we can see lived out today, as you read this book, wherever you are in the world.

One is for a man to dig in his heels and reassert his traditional male identity. Such a man usually has very negative feelings towards the changing role of women. He values ruggedness, endurance, and being muscular, and disdains the thought of being feminized, labeling such a man as a "pussy."

The second possible reaction is for men to apologize or to feel ashamed of their masculinity and to become overly feminized. This is a man who talks a lot about his feelings, who emphasizes harmony, and who is soft and gentle. He participates fully in the affairs of the house; he is a caring and attentive father. But, as we will discover in this book, he may also lose his sense of confidence and "mission," which can be central to a man's sense of wellbeing. To his surprise, expressing passion often disappears in his relationship to be replaced with becoming friendly roommates.

The third possible reaction is to try to ignore gender differences altogether. Courses in many universities today teach students that gender is all a social construct, that there is no real difference between men and women. We would agree that rigid gender rules and stereotyping from the past are indeed a social construct. At the same time, this is a very unwise position that ignores the fact that we are different. Increasing amounts of research shows that there are real biological and hormonal differences that determine how men and women react to life's challenges very differently. It is that difference that creates diversity, and through diversity, we create something that is greater than the sum of its parts.

The fourth possibility is what this book is about. It is the exercise of conscious choice. A Conscious Man is not a slave to biology. He is aware of the balance between masculine and feminine energy within himself, but the way that he lives with each is determined by awareness more than by automatic reactions to anything external. A Conscious Man has a sense of the vast variety of different roles he can enjoy in his life. He is aware of our history and how dramatically things have changed for him in the last few years. He responds to life not only as a duty to fulfill but also as an art to create.

MASCULINE AND FEMININE ENERGY

Almost everybody on the planet is born either as a man or as a woman. It is a clearly defined difference of gender for 1,999 out of 2,000 newborn babies. Physically, it is a simple description: a man (a male human being) has a penis, testicles, and a flat chest. He also has a prostate gland, a deeper voice, and facial hair. A woman, on the other hand (who is female), has a vagina, ovaries, and breasts. She has a menstrual cycle which begins at puberty and ends in menopause, and she is capable of bearing children. These are entirely physical differences between men and women.

At the same time, these physical differences create biochemical and hormonal differences in the body. We will talk about these a lot in this book. The primary and most relevant difference is that both men and women, particularly today, experience stress. This idea can be condensed to dealing with difficult challenges, often under time pressure, in a way that does not fully allow us the possibility of bringing everything to a resolution. The biochemical experience of stress in men and women is the same: it involves the secretion of adrenalin and cortisol into the bloodstream at a faster rate than can be neutralized. But the way that men and women deal with stress, and therefore come back to balance and wellbeing, is different.

Men counter stress hormones through the release of testosterone. Some studies have indicated that men have as much as thirty times more testosterone in their blood than women do. Testosterone is a hormone associated with having the courage and determination to meet difficult challenges, to push through and complete them, and to do so with faster reaction time. Women, on the other hand, balance stress through the secretion of oxytocin, sometimes known as the "feel-good" hormone. Oxytocin is released when women can be relational without having to solve any problem or discuss any specific agenda. When women get together with other women to talk, laugh, and share their feelings, there is an immediate surge in oxytocin, and stress is neutralized.

Although our roles in society have changed dramatically in the last decades, the way that our nervous systems work and the way that hormones are released in the body do not change so quickly. It takes generations for genetics to even begin to catch up with changes in our environment.

In this book, we will also refer to another distinction, besides male and female bodies, which has more to do with energy or qualities. We call this "masculine" and "feminine." We have both been working with people in this area for decades, so we have had the opportunity to ask countless people what they understand by these words. There is not much variation in people's responses.

The word "masculine" is generally used to refer to an energetic disposition which is focused, goal oriented, centered, and present and thrusts into the future. In China, masculine energy is associated with the yang quality; in India it is associated with Shiva; and Jung called it the "animus." Feminine energy, on the other hand, is widely recognized to be embracing, receiving, soft, nurturing, loving, and relational. In China, the feminine is associated with yin; in India it is known as Shakti; and Jung would refer to it as the "anima."

While almost everybody is biologically born male or female, people today in many different disciplines are recognizing that both men and women have access to masculine and feminine energy. In many ways, it is finding the correct balance between these two energies, for you as a unique individual, that determines how good you feel about yourself and how good you feel about your life.

The balance of masculine and feminine energy is determined by many factors. To some degree it is genetic. Some men are just born very masculine: they are often more burly, more hairy, more determined, and more action oriented. Some other men, who are equally men, are just born with slightly more feminine energy as well: they tend to notice the aesthetics of their environment more, and they are more relational and more sensitive in all sorts of ways. The same is true for women. Some women are born with more feminine energy, and some women have more of a balance of masculine energy.

This balance of masculine and feminine energy is not just genetic. It is also affected by childhood conditioning. If a little boy is raised by a single mother with two or three sisters in the house, for example, his environment may skew him more towards the feminine. He may equally rebel against his conditioning, when he gets to be a teen, and become a macho guy.

A third important way that we get conditioned around the balance of masculine and feminine energy comes from ideology. Because everything we are talking about here is so much up in the air, there are a-million-and-one theories about how a man and how a woman should be. One book may tell you to increase your masculine energy so you can polarize with the feminine. Another book may tell you to find a balance of masculine and feminine energy within yourself.

A Conscious Man is one who is aware of his natural character and can recognize the way that he was born. He is aware of his true nature and has no reason to suppress it. He is also conscious of the different kinds of conditioning that have influenced him, and this awareness also gives him the possibility of conscious choice. His masculinity is not simply an automatic enactment of his biology or the different voices that have told him how he should be. His masculinity has become something like a work of art: a conscious gift to the world that allows him to be fully himself, to lean into his strengths, and to contribute fully to everyone he influences.

Consciousness changes everything. Almost anything you can possibly do or say will be experienced very differently whether it is done automatically or consciously. A simple example of this would be anger. When anger takes you over, it can easily be ugly and become violent. The great majority of the things we regret doing or saying happened when we were angry. It can be difficult to repair the damage done in such moments. But this does not mean that expressing anger is always destructive. If you were faced with an adult hurting a child, or had the opportunity to intervene in some of the huge social injustices in the world, the conscious expression of anger could be the greatest contribution you could make. The difference is that it is given consciously. Anything given consciously rather than automatically is transformed through that awareness.

A Conscious Man is not a superior man. He is not more evolved or more accomplished. He is certainly not richer or more virile or more powerful. He does not have bigger muscles or a hairier chest or a faster car. The Conscious Man, in the way we use the term, simply means a man who has put some attention, and therefore some choice, into the expression of his masculinity. He is living his art rather than his automation.

WHY WE WROTE THIS BOOK

This book is not intended to be theoretical, but practical. We feel that there are a number of simple things that a man can recognize about himself, which radically increases his sense of his wellbeing as well as his positive impact on those around him. We hope to offer something here which will allow you the possibility of greater freedom of choice.

We have had the opportunity to ask men what most significantly contributes to feeling comfortable within their own skin. But equally, we have asked women what they appreciate about men. We have focused here on the twelve most important qualities we see as being characteristic of conscious masculinity. Not every man is going to equally display all of these qualities. In fact, a man might be very conscious of himself yet might be missing some of the masculine qualities completely. He just might not have chosen to develop them.

Each chapter is divided into four sections. First, we define the quality and explore the biology. Then we discuss what gets in the way of its development. Then we also offer practical tools. And finally, we have some suggestions to women for what they can do to bring forth each masculine quality more in a man.

The Quality. We start by mapping what each quality is and how it is connected to biology. Here you can decide if this is a quality of Conscious Masculinity that feels important to you. If you know that it is already fully developed in your life, then celebrate it. If you know that you could develop this more, as an art form, then read on.

What Gets in the Way. Here, we explore the hero's journey you will need to take to develop each masculine quality. We are all subject to layers of conditioning that often make it hard to bring forth the best of what we have to give, some of which can be painful. Think of these obstacles as parts of you that can sabotage and cause havoc if you are unaware of them, but can become helpful or even humorous when brought out of the shadows. The key in reading this section of each chapter is mindfulness. Simply to be aware of unconscious habits that may go back several generations in your family diminishes their power more than trying to get rid of anything or to blame yourself in any way.

The Practices. In each chapter, we also offer practical tools, things you can do starting today, to increase that particular quality in a way that is not only obvious to you subjectively but that can also be felt by other people.

For Women. Finally, we are very aware that conscious masculinity is a subject that is not only interesting to men. Women all over the world frequently ask us "Where do I find a Conscious Man?" In each section, we address this: if you are in a relationship, how can you best support your partner to bring forth that particular quality? If you are single, this section discusses why a man who already displays this particular quality may make a good partner for you.

We do not claim to be the ultimate authority on manhood. We simply aim to offer you the benefit of our many decades of combined experience in this area and our seeing how needlessly many men and women suffer simply from not understanding their biology. We cannot know every aspect of what it means to be a man, so please take what helps and leave the rest. For example, we are both straight men. Neither of us have had any gay experience. It would be pure arrogance on our part to start professing how gay men should conduct relationships. Therefore, this book is primarily written for heterosexual men. If you are a gay man, welcome. Come on in. Please take what you can that is helpful for you, and please excuse the fact that we have not addressed gay relationships because it is just not what we are good at.

In addition, we happen to both be in happy monogamous relationships. John has been married to Bonnie for thirty years, Arjuna has been married to Chameli for thirteen, and we celebrate monogamy. But we are equally aware that there are many ways to live a happy life, and there is no absolute right or wrong. Some people today are exploring polyamory: having multiple partners. Others have decided to stay single and have isolated sexual experiences with different people. And others chose to not be sexual at all. This is a book primarily about heterosexual monogamous men because that is what we know about from our own experience and what we have supported other men in to live successfully. Please take what you can, and translate it into your view.

With all of that said, lets jump in to the first and perhaps the most important aspect of being a Conscious Man: his sense of mission and purpose.

Chapter One

HE KNOWS HIS MISSION AND PURPOSE

In all of the research and interviews we did in preparing to write this book, we found that the single most important factor that allows a man to feel comfortable and strong within himself is having a strong and clear sense of his mission and purpose. This is the "make or break" factor of conscious masculinity.

When a Conscious Man knows his place in the world — what he has to contribute — this naturally overflows into being a more present and loving partner and father to his children. Once he finds his mission, he can share it in relationship, but when he is rooted deeply in his masculine essence, a relationship for its own sake will be secondary to his mission. Most men create stronger bonds and lasting friendships with other men when they have a shared sense of something that they can accomplish together.

Contemporary man faces an interesting and unprecedented dilemma, one that our male ancestors have never faced before in this same way. If we go just back just a few generations, all over the world, it was very clear what you were going to do with your life. In almost every case, you would do what your father had done before you. If your father was a carpenter, you would become a carpenter. If you were the son of a writer, you became a writer. If you were the son of the king, you would in turn become the king. There was not much of a decision to be made. Even if you did not follow exactly in your father's footsteps, the circumstances of your birth would determine a very narrow scope of what was available to you. Today, a man has a much greater opportunity than ever before to do what he wants: become a lawyer or a doctor or a musician or a writer or even the president of a country.

This is a great blessing because it gives us all greater freedom and opportunity. But it also presents a new dilemma that previous generations have never faced before. It is the huge and sometimes burdensome question of "What should I do with my life? What is my purpose?" Today, there are all kinds of workshops, seminars, and books dedicated to supporting people to find their purpose. This is a strictly modern preoccupation. It is not something for which we have much precedent in the past. It can easily create a sense of panic in modern man, a fear that if he does not get it right, something terrible will happen.

In India, there was a word for this sense of your inherited place in society. It was called your "dharma." Another Arjuna, 5000 years ago, was faced with a terrifying predicament in the Kurushetra Battle: whether to fight, which would involve killing his own family members, or whether to back away, which would be seen as an ignobility worse than death. Because he was in the warrior class, there was really no choice but to do his duty, the one he was born into.

Men today dance between two opposing forces. On the one hand is the momentum of the hyper-masculine trance: do your duty — fight the war — whether you believe in it or not. Do what you are told. Don't ask questions. The alternative appears to be breaking free of what is expected of you and being sensitive to what feels good instead. A man can ask himself, "What gives me pleasure?" "What would I really like to do?" This kind of sensitivity puts him more into his feminine side, which can easily cause him to feel ungrounded, uncentered, and then lost and confused.

Conscious Dharma

Many men today are discovering a way to transcend and integrate this dilemma: we call it "Conscious Dharma." It means not just to do what your father did or what is expected of you by other people, but not to get lost in fleeting feelings that come and go. Conscious Dharma means to drop much deeper into yourself to a place where you know the Right Thing To Do. This means the actions and disposition that work best not only for you but for everybody else involved as well. Sometimes discovering Conscious Dharma might mean that you take care of your family, your immediate environment, and perhaps also a few other people in your close vicinity. For others, finding your Conscious Dharma might mean slipping into a role that fulfills the needs of millions of people: if you discover that your destiny happens to be writing a best-selling book or being world-class musician. The scope of your influence, or the conventional measures of worldly success, do not matter nearly as much as finding your right place.

Everybody we interviewed for this book has discovered this sense of Conscious Dharma, and they described it in almost identical ways. It feels like you have been taken over by a force bigger than your own mind and emotions. One man said, "It is how the Great Spirit expresses itself through you in a way that it could not express itself through anyone else. It's a unique flavor, a song that only you can sing when you relax and allow yourself to completely be yourself. Because of its uniqueness, there is actually a duty, an obligation to show up. If you flake out, no one else can steward this particular gift for you."

Conscious Dharma is an integration of masculine and feminine energies within a man. The masculine part of him has a vision and a purpose and can put aside and sacrifice immediate pleasure for a bigger and more important outcome. Accessing feminine energy within himself allows him to experience passion—to follow his bliss. He has not become feminine, but he has become sensitive to the balance of these two energies in a skillful way that allows him to become integrated and whole.

Get Inspired

The quickest way to fall into your Conscious Dharma is through inspiration. It happens when you recognize other people who inspire you deeply, and it happens during the moments in your own life when you feel most inspired and alive. This is when you become a "man on fire." When these things happen, a vision crystallizes of the right use of your life where everything falls into place.

The way that we wrote this book together is a great example of living in this way. We created this book through hours and hours of dialogues at John's home in Mill Valley. Arjuna came to stay for a few days at a time, and then we would hang out together in John's office (something like a little cave dug into the hillside) or go for walks in the California sunshine with John's dog. Many days we would be up with the sunrise, drink a quick smoothie for breakfast, and start our talks for the book at 7 a.m. We would go right through the day, and still be at it, energized and inspired at 11 or 12 at night. This process was more or less effortless for us. Subjectively, it just felt like we were having a great time doing what we most love with a close friend. At the same time, we were creating a book that we hope will serve many people.

This is the key not only to building fantastic friendships with other men but also to living a life of vision. Let yourself become inspired by a long-term vision with an outcome that can have the greatest benefit for as many people as possible. Then plan each day around how to execute it.

When you discover your sense of Conscious Dharma, all the lights on your Christmas tree go on at once: everything falls into place. The people we interviewed for this book all experience a sense of having almost limitless energy. They can often work fourteen or sixteen hour days, but it feels more like play than work. They have relatively little stress. In fact, once you fall into this way of living, you understand that stress is a byproduct of doing things that are not right for you. For both of us (we both travel and teach seminars around the world), when we are living our purpose fully, it generates a sense of wellbeing unlike anything else. The idea of retirement becomes quite meaningless once you discover your Conscious Dharma. You can retire from a job. But once you are lucky enough to find what you do in the world as a perfect expression of your unique gifts and talents, you will never retire until your last breath.

Never about the Money

A Conscious Man does not make major life decisions based on money although he absolutely has to handle money consciously and clearly so he can fully devote himself to Doing the Right Thing. We will hear from John

Mackey, the founder of Whole Foods, who has not taken any money out of his business as salary, stock options, or bonuses for eight years. He works completely out of a sense of mission. But he is only able to do that because he has already put his financial affairs in order. People who have discovered their right place in the world say that it feels quite selfless, not something you do to get money but something that often generates money as a byproduct.

John says: I've been traveling to China frequently lately to teach seminars to large numbers of people. It's a sixteen-hour flight, which I'd much prefer not to have to do. I don't particularly enjoy sitting in a tiny little cabin where the air is really bad, the food is awful, and I feel cramped. I go to China not because I enjoy to travel but because it is an opportunity to live my mission. For sure, I get well paid, which is a way for me to know that I'm being valued. But if I were getting paid to fly to China to meet one person, I wouldn't do it. It's because I'm reaching a lot of people and making a big difference that I find this so fulfilling. The hardest times for me actually are when I don't have anything to do. When I take a few weeks off, I can get lethargic and a little depressed. I need something to get me out of bed. When my wife calls me and asks for help with something then, boom, I'm right there. As a man, I need that sense of mission.

Initially, rediscovering your sense of Conscious Dharma may be a challenging process. As we said already, the sense of panic that many men face can be overwhelming and immobilizing. We need to start with small steps. But we also need to be awake and ready to face what gets in the way. This may start out as a fairly mental and deliberate process of experimenting with specific practices that reconnect you with your sense of purpose. Once it starts to kick in, you know it, and you feel it in your whole body. It can become a positive addiction! As soon as you find your place in the world, it feels like your hand is slipping into a perfectly fitting glove. Stress melts away in those moments, and you feel carried by the force that gives us all life.

We are going to guide you through a number of specific practices that will help you to reconnect to yourself and to live in this way. But first, it is important to face the forces that still have some control over most of us as men, that get in the way of finding our Conscious Dharma.

WHAT GETS IN THE WAY

Often, you do not need to do anything about old, automatic habits. You simply need to be fully present with them and aware of them, and magically, the poison is removed from the fangs of the viper. Fighting obstacles often makes them stronger. That is why we called this book "Conscious Men," and not "Improved Men" or "Accomplished Men." Mindfulness is the key to everything. It causes distractions to dissolve on their own and brings forth the light of your true magnificence to the surface. These habits are like "parts of you" that have been split off and disowned. Hence, we give each one a name.

Conformist Colin

In order to discover your Conscious Dharma, you first need to be aware of all the unconscious forces that influence you. What did your father expect you to do? And your mother? Where do you feel obligated by your education? What do your friends think is the cool thing to do?

Arjuna says: I remember when my oldest son Abhi went off to university. He was all set to become a film director. I was thrilled. I had always wanted to do that myself but then went in another direction. Eventually, he realized that his real passion was more with the exploration of wellness than with film, and he changed his degree to holistic health. He had been swayed in his choice of degree by his father's influence, in a way that was unconscious to both him and to me. Abhi had to go through an inner struggle to become aware of unconscious forces and assumptions imposed by his dad that were influencing his choices.

Greedy George

We are all being so hypnotized, particularly in America, by images of what money and being famous can do for us. We all grew up on television programs like *Lifestyles of the Rich and Famous*. Every time you go to pay for your groceries in the supermarket, you are faced with an array of magazines blaring images of celebrities living in mansions. Recently, a number of successful and wealthy actors like Sean Penn, Russell Brand, and Brad Pitt have given interviews talking about what an empty goal the whole pursuit had been. Interestingly, these actors went on to put their energy into social and political action. We all have to face these kinds of strong temptations and drop deeper into our true calling.

The key to getting free from letting money drive your life is to introduce the word "enough" into your vocabulary. In one study, researchers discovered that wellbeing and money relate to each other on a bell curve. If you are only earning $25,000 a year, and your income goes up to $30,000, it is likely that your wellbeing will increase. This stays true up to around $100,000 a year, and then it levels off. Extra money past that point makes very little difference to enjoying your life. The researchers also discovered something fascinating: the bell curve starts to drop off on the other side. When income goes up from $200,000 to $300,000 a year, the average sense of wellbeing starts to decline.

Maybe you know the story of Paul Getty, who was at one time the richest man in the world. He was visiting London and rented the entire top floor of the Hyde Park Hilton. A journalist with the *London Times* went to interview him. "Mr. Getty," he asked, "You are the richest man in the world. When is enough enough?"

Getty had to think for a few minutes, but finally, he answered, "Not quite yet."

That is how it is with money and fame. Neither one truly fulfills you, so it always seems like just a little bit more will do the trick. The key to breaking the trance is to get to a place of "enough" and then to enjoy it and focus on what you have to contribute.

Instant Gratification Ian

Another habit we need to face in returning to a true sense of mission and purpose is too much emphasis on what feels good in a fleeting way. The whole idea of "follow your bliss" and trying to find out what gives you the most pleasure, moment to moment, can become more of a distraction to a deeper sense of why you are really here than a path to it. Sometimes we have to sacrifice immediate pleasure for a deeper sense of mission, like John on his long flights to China, but the rewards are much greater.

Distracted Dominic

All of us live today in a culture that fosters endless distraction. Advertisers continually jostle with each other for our attention. Watching TV and cruising the Internet can easily distract your brain in a way that can cause you to lose focus and that deeper sense of why you are alive. Stepping away from your mission and purpose does not feel good, so it is natural to want to blunt that feeling of suffering. This leads to an even greater craving for distraction, always wanting more. The simplest way to cut through the fog of distraction is to make sure that you punctuate your life with periods of stillness to observe what is going on inside of you.

Fearful Frank

You need to take care of your basic survival needs in order to create enough space to discover your Conscious Dharma. If you are hungry, and you do not know where your next meal is coming from, or if you do not have money for rent, that preoccupation is bound to eclipse a more expansive sense of service.

John says: I remember how I got started doing my thing. I had spent the most of my 20s living in a meditation center in Switzerland. Then I heard that my younger brother Jimmy was having a very hard time; he suffered from bipolar disorder. I came back to Texas to see him. Teaching him meditation was not enough. So I went to California to find other ways to help him. I went to a few weekend seminars, and right away, I had the thought, *Hey I could do this.* How do you start? But I also had to earn a living. I was homeless at that time, sleeping on the beach. I asked my mother for help. She paid for a computer programming training course. I got my credential in six months, and one of my other brothers offered me a job at the Stanford Research Institute. Somewhere, deep inside, I knew I did not want to spend the rest of my life as a computer programmer. I felt inspired by the seminars I had been to and by the thought of helping my brother. I saved all the money I made, and I wrote my first book in my spare time. Then came *Men Are from Mars, Women Are from Venus,* and I was able to live my Conscious Dharma full time.

Jimmy shot himself. It was the greatest tragedy of my life. I wasn't able to help him in time. But it became a wakeup call for me. Jimmy did me the greatest service. He pulled me out of a life that was just about meditation and going inward and gave me the inspiration to serve other people. Once I had that inspiration, I needed that intermediary step of taking care of money to be able to finally devote myself to my reason for being on the planet. My brother Jimmy has been the inspiration and motivation for all these decades to help people alleviate unnecessary suffering. I dedicate my work to him.

Oversight Oliver

Once you fall into this sense of the Right Thing to Do, you discover that your right place in the world was staring you in the face the whole time. When a baby laughs, when a cat stretches, when a bird flaps its wings, they are all living their Dharma. It is effortless and natural. The only thing you need to do to come back to that sense of purpose is to become aware of what gets in the way. You don't always need to know cognitively what your mission is. You only need to know what it isn't, and then what is left will flow on its own.

THE PRACTICES

Researchers like Elizabeth Kubler-Ross tell us that people who have a "near death experience" often describe seeing their whole life flash before their eyes. They realize that they had been chasing all the wrong dreams. Later, they stop pursuing money and fame and find that making the greatest contribution is the reward they were looking for, not the money that it brings. You can come to that same clarity without having to risk your life or to die temporarily. This means to question all the false identities that have been embossed into your soul by culture, family, and philosophies, both ancient and modern. It means to become aware of them and to let them go. Then your innocent face, your natural voice, emerges, and you know the Right Thing to Do.

Journaling

A great way to get started with this is by keeping a journal. For example, you can write a list of all the people in the world who most inspire you. Take the time to really go into this deeply. Whose life story lights you up with a sense of energy and passion? Once you have collected some names like this, scan the list and think about the qualities that each person emanates rather than the specific activities they are involved in.

For example:

Leonard Cohen ~ Poetic visionary

Paul McCartney ~ Heartfelt creative genius

Eckhart Tolle ~ Natural authentic mystic

John Mackey ~ Conscious entrepreneur

Barbara Marx Hubbard ~ Energized aging

Oprah Winfrey ~ Generous change agent

Steve Jobs ~ Persistent innovator

Malala Yousafzai ~ Courageous rebel

Muhamed Yunus ~ Empowering leader

The next step is to envision a life for yourself that allows you to live these same qualities. Perhaps you can think of some activities that are available to you right away, today, that can allow you to explore these qualities more fully.

You can also ask twelve people for the qualities they most admire in you. Ask people who have known you for a long time like your brothers and sisters or childhood friends. If you ask twelve people to tell you twelve qualities they each admire and appreciate about you, you will get 144 qualities in all. You will find that many people will list qualities that are very similar, so you can group these together. This is probably the surest and most reliable way to get a sense of your "unique energetic blueprint." For example, after doing such an exercise, you might have a list that includes insightful, humorous, articulate, focused, inspiring, and artful as a leader. Now, in the same way as above, you can journal about the kinds of activities that are immediately available to you to explore those qualities more. This can naturally lead to the next step: developing a vision of a way of life based around those qualities. Arjuna says: You can read more about this process, which we call "Midwifing the Unique Gift" in my book *Better Than Sex*.

Peer Support and Mentoring

The unconscious masculine, out of which we are all evolving, has had a tendency to isolate himself, to have the thought *I have to do this all on my own*. Another man, whether a professional coach or simply a close friend, can help you to create the much needed ingredient of accountability.

Here is how it works. Once you have a sense of the qualities that most inspire you, or indeed the qualities that other people most appreciate about you, carve out small periods every day that you can devote to developing these qualities. This process of carving out a little time each day takes discipline, and discipline is infinitely easier to find in collaboration with other men than it is on your own. An accountability partner is simply somebody you report to every day to say whether you did what you said you would do or not. A daily email will suffice quite well.

Break it down into tiny steps. For example, commit to working on your book (or whatever it is) for just ten minutes a day. Ten minutes is easy. After ten minutes, if you feel like continuing, great. But your commitment is actually only for ten minutes. Then send your accountability partner an email saying, "Yes I did it." If you don't trust yourself to tell the truth about this, which some people don't, you could email proof of what you accomplished that day. You and your buddy will find between yourselves the best ways to hold each other accountable.

The Vision Quest

Here is a very powerful way (and you could say a foolproof way) to bring forth a sense of mission.

Arjuna says: As an Awakening Coach, whenever I work with a man who feels that he has lost his sense of mission and purpose, I do everything I can to support him to take a retreat alone. Five days is ideal, but take as long as you can manage. You need to minimize all distractions, so switch off the phone, leave the computer at home, no reading, and no writing. The key to a retreat like this is the quality of waiting. I have suggested such a retreat to dozens of men over the last 25 years of coaching. Some said that it felt like going crazy: every kind of weird, exaggerated fantasy floats before your eyes. But as each one floats in, you can have the intelligence to let it go and recognize that it is just the conditioned mind. Almost invariably, by the end, you find that your head is clear. All the fears and desires have dissipated and are recognized just as thoughts, and then you just know what to do. You absolutely know what was your distraction in your life, and you absolutely know what your true calling is.

I suggested this retreat to one man who was living in New York and working as a hedge fund manager. He was making a multiple six-figure income, and he was engaged to be married. By the end of the retreat, he just knew what to do. He drove back to New York and went almost directly to his fiancée's house. "I'm sorry," he said, "I know this is difficult and painful for both of us, but I've realized that I'm not the right man to make you happy. We really wouldn't be right for each other. And also, I have realized that the work I've been doing is not really my passion at all; I was doing it just for the money." Of course, they had to talk things through, but finally, he left New York and went back to his native Australia to do what really inspired him the most: surfing. He opened a shop on the beach selling surfboards and went on to found a very successful surfboard manufacturing company. If he hadn't gone on that five-day retreat, his life would have taken a very different turn.

Celebrate Your Victories

Another important practice in bringing forth your true sense of purpose is to celebrate victories. When you have accomplished something great, create the time to be with your children or your partner to really enjoy the other aspects of your life that are not the primary expressions of your mission. A Conscious Man needs work time as well as cake time: Mission Time as well as Mission Accomplished Time.

John says: At the end of the day, I love to have dinner with Bonnie, my wife, and then we sit on the couch and watch television. After a day of giving everything I have to give, I feel like I've earned the right to sit here. I've done my duty. If I had not done all I could to serve people in the day, I would not be able to enjoy this downtime so much.

FOR WOMEN

Sometimes women ask us, in one-on-one sessions or in seminars, how they can best support a man to connect more deeply with his sense of purpose. Here are some tips that have proven useful to some women and to the men they love.

It makes all the difference to a man for you to understand just how central it is to his sense of wellbeing and identity to have a sense of mission and purpose. Of course, as a woman, you have a sense of mission and purpose as well, but it is different for men. They take it much more personally.

If a man says to a woman, "You look beautiful today," or if he complements her on what she is wearing, her hair, or any other aspect of her beauty, she will generally involuntarily flush, smile, and feel nourished. The feminine in all of us (both men and women) is more identified with radiance and beauty. On the other hand, if you say to a man, "Wow, that is a really beautiful T-shirt," he is likely to shrug and grunt, "Uh, thanks. I guess." In fact, he might want to take the shirt off and give it to you because the masculine energy in all of us is more identified with making a difference in some action-oriented way.

If you tell a man that his accomplishments are meaningless or a waste of time, he will generally feel that his identity is under attack. Tell him that you are impressed with what he has accomplished, the way he has rebuilt his computer or his shed, and he will feel that you "get" him totally. Both men and women have mission, and both men and women can look good, but for him, his mission is closely tied to his identity: he takes it very personally.

Encourage Him

One of the wounds that men suffer from is that they had dreams when they were young: "I want to be a doctor. I want to be a lawyer." If his mother made fun of his dreams, it becomes a wound he carries later. A mother who says, "That's a great idea, honey," is more likely to foster a sense of inspiration and "I can do it" in her son. It is possible that your partner may still be carrying such wounds. Listening to his dreams and believing in them will bring forth the best in him.

John says: Sometimes I get a check in the mail with some extra unexpected money. Then Bonnie says, "Oh, it's great. You made all that money." It gave me a moment of pleasure. A few minutes later, I might be making eggs for breakfast. I make exceptionally good fried eggs: I steam them in a little water in the bottom of the pan. When Bonnie talks about how good my eggs are, that gives me even more pleasure. She brags about my eggs to our guests. Whether I make good eggs does not makes much difference to her practically, much less than the money. But it gives me much greater emotional fulfillment when she complements my eggs. I thrive on her encouragement, often in small things.

Encouraging a man does not mean giving suggestions of what he should do or pointing out where he is a failure. Wait until he comes up with a dream, an aspiration, and then do not step on it! Men generally experience any kind of suggestion as nagging, or pressuring, and it shuts down their creativity.

You may have seen movies where women get together and make fun of their men. Because some women see men as having an obsession with accomplishment and actions, which do not necessarily mean so much to them, it is natural to laugh together about how seriously men take their sense of mission and even to belittle them behind their backs. If you do this with other women when you get home, your man's achievements may seem much less significant.

Arjuna says: When I'm busy writing books and coaching, and generally feeling all puffed up about being on my mission, I get very lazy about the kitchen. I walk in and grab something with the thought that I'll clean it all up later. Chameli doesn't like it. She'll often come in and clean up after me but then feel resentful. This doesn't work well for either of us. She has learned over our many years of being together to do it in a slightly different way. She just has to ask me: "Would you mind cleaning the kitchen?" or "I'd really appreciate if you take out the garbage." By telling me clearly what action she wants me to take that will make her happy, it gives me a sense of the right thing to do, and that reconnects me with the feeling of being in my dharma. She gets a clean kitchen, and I get that inexpressibly good feeling of being a man with purpose.

Looking for Mr. Right

If you are single and want to bring the right conscious man into your life, it is a great idea to recognize the distinction between a man who makes money and a man who has a strong sense of mission and purpose for which money is a byproduct. A man who is financially secure will bring more respect and balance to your life in the long run. But to create a lasting, stable, and happy relationship, it is much more important that he has a strong sense of mission and purpose, and that the money is a secondary thing. A man who knows he is doing good in the world is also more likely to be a loving, caring, and attentive partner, a good father, a better lover, more humorous, and less stressed.

In coaching couples, we have both seen that for many women, a Conscious Man can easily get confused in her mind with the old hyper-masculine trance. You may misinterpret the Conscious Man as being old-fashioned, self-centered, arrogant, or unloving because his life is about mission, working hard, and solving problems. But there is a big difference, as we will see in the rest of the book. A Conscious Man is not addicted to doing. He also knows how to take space when he needs to and to let it all go. His heart is becoming more open every day as he is learning how to love deeply. We will find out more about these things in the chapters that follow.

A CONSCIOUS MAN:

MEET JOHN MACKEY, FOUNDER OF WHOLE FOODS

Every man has to find his mission and calling — his higher purpose. That does not necessarily mean that you are called to change the world. Rather, it is what resonates with your heart, your inner being. Initially for me, it was just about selling healthy food to people, earning a living, and having some fun. But my mission has unfolded and evolved over time and continues to.

When you have things that you are creatively involved in, that you care about, that are true to your passions, your life becomes far more interesting, far more exciting. And when you're more fully engaged, you have more vitality. I've taken lots of vacations, and traveled the world, but for me that leisure time is primarily about re-creation so that I can revitalize myself and go back to fulfilling my higher purpose in life. If I had to do it all over again, I would make the same choices.

When I was in college, I didn't like a particular book I was reading, but it was required to finish the course. I stood up one day, threw the book on the ground, and said, "I'm not going to read this anymore," and then I dropped all the classes I wasn't really enjoying. That choice has defined the rest of my life. Life is too short to do things that aren't aligned with who I am.

If you want to find your purpose in life, start by being true to yourself. Your purpose is within your own being—it's imprinted in the deepest part of you. Although we can tap into this purpose, most of us don't listen to it because we are afraid. We are afraid of rejection, failure, and poverty; afraid of being laughed at and not being loved; sometimes we're even afraid of our own potential greatness, a greatness we don't feel worthy of.

Whole Foods started because I followed my own heart, my own curiosity. When we act—and actively choose—to follow our hearts, the world conspires to help us: we meet the right people, things happen at the right time, happy coincidences unfold all around us. When you commit, the universe rearranges itself to have those dreams—your dreams—fulfilled.

When you are on your path, it leads to service. As you grow as a spiritual human being, the ego lessens and service grows. To be the leader I wanted to be, I stopped taking money. I haven't taken any compensation from Whole Foods now in eight years. Instead, I donate what would be my stock options to my foundations. I am the father of Whole Foods, and like a parent I now serve the company and don't get paid for it. Like a parent, I do it out of love. Just as parents want their children to flourish, I want Whole Foods to flourish, and knowing the company and the people working there are flourishing brings me immense joy.

Business truly has to be a win-win-win situation. Everyone exchanging with a business is doing so for their own mutual benefit. There are six major stakeholders who we consciously attempt to make happy at Whole Foods: customers, employees, suppliers, investors, the community, and the planet. We consciously attempt to create value for all these different, independent stakeholders as well. People tend to think in trade-offs: "If you're doing this for your stockholders, then it must be coming at the expense of your employees." If you live for trade-offs, you'll find them, but if you look for synergies, you'll find them. Whenever I have to make a big decision, I always ask myself, "Are any of the stakeholders losing?" If so, it's probably not the right decision.

Chapter Two

HE TAKES SPACE GRACEFULLY

I f we go back a few thousand years, just the blink of an eye in the history of our species, men and women lived very different lives. In most parts of the world, men would go out to hunt for food aiming to capture and kill wild animals — a dangerous business. It required the immediate ability to either muster all your strength and courage and wits to fight, or if the odds were against you, to run as fast as you could up the nearest tree. This kind of lifestyle, which went on uninterrupted for thousands of years, required a man to build up, and then store, and then release testosterone into his bloodstream. Testosterone allowed him to meet each challenge courageously and to see it through to completion.

Meanwhile, because of their biological capacity to bear children, women would stay home during the day nursing the smallest children, watching over the growing siblings to make sure they came to no harm, and keeping an eye out for snakes and scorpions. She kept the home clean and comfortable and prepared food while at the same time lending an ear to her neighbors and their troubles and triumphs. None of this was particularly dangerous, relative to what the men were doing, so it allowed for a much more relaxed and social contact, mostly with other women. And it also required her to spread her attention around in order to do many things at once.

At night, the men came home. After the evening meal, it was time to sit around the fire. Even today, among indigenous people, men and women each have their own fire some distance apart from each other.

The women's fire is an animated place: they laugh about stories of the day and rub each others' shoulders and feet. They bond by connecting with each other in a relaxed way, without any agenda, thereby releasing the stress of having so many things to do simultaneously during the day. The woman gets replenished and then has more love to give to her family and community the next day.

The men's fire is a very different scene. A man sits or squats, staring into the fire. There is relatively little talking, except perhaps one man telling the story of great feats of heroes from the past while the other men silently listen. He might sharpen his tools or simply stare blankly into the fire. He is not doing anything but is also not sleeping. This combination of stillness, listening, and alertness, is what is required for him to come back to a feeling of centeredness, reconnection with himself, and a restored capacity to meet the challenges of his life with focus.

For thousands of years, women have come back to themselves, returning to love and feeling comfortable within their own skin through connection with other women. They do so through caring and listening and sharing and talking and laughing and giving friendly, reassuring touches. Men have come back to themselves — returning to centeredness — through silence, stillness, and spaciousness either in solitude or a fairly structured way of being with other men.

The lifestyles and the kinds of challenges that men and women face today could not be more different to what we have faced historically, while at the same time, our nervous systems have not been rewired as quickly.

Unconscious, instinctive drives still cause a woman to seek security and protection from a man and cause a man to want sex and progeny from a woman. But as men and women both become more conscious, they mature beyond these instinctive short-term drives that are generated from the back part of the brain (reptilian) to more conscious choices for long-term fulfillment that are generated from the pre-frontal cortex.

The Quest for Wholeness

Today, both men and women want to experience a multidimensional, fulfilled life: they both want to have interesting jobs and careers, they both want to create long-term satisfying relationships, they both want to create and participate in a happy family life, they both want great sex, and they both want to experience balance and wellbeing.

A man today does not want to be restricted to going out and facing dangerous challenges during the day and then staring into a fire at night. He has claimed his right to participate more fully in family life. Modern man wants to be there for the birth of his children, and he wants to be there as a fully engaged father, fully involved in birthdays and sports events, school plays, and field trips. He wants to be a part of making the home beautiful and preparing and cooking great food. He is choosing, consciously, to expand into living all parts of himself.

We see the same shift even in his emotional and sexual life. Only a few decades back, most men experienced romantic feelings and the need to bond emotionally primarily during the courtship phase. This is when he had a challenge, a mission to accomplish. Men might write poetry, give roses, and feel deeply romantic feelings…up until when his prize was secure, he had slipped the ring onto her finger, and soon after gotten her pregnant. Afterwards, his romantic feelings would often quickly diminish. Once the challenge of the situation had passed, he would frequently get interested in other women and have affairs, secretly or overtly, to again stimulate his love of the challenge.

The Conscious Man recognizes that these hyper-masculine behaviors, despite the fact that they have been time tested over such a long period, do not give him everything he longs for. Today, men marry for love and aspire to create lasting and fulfilling relationships. In addition, more men today are choosing monogamy as a value, not as a moral dictate. Many men in the past used to get married for convenience. Our literature is littered with stories of a man who had romantic feelings for one woman but finally had to marry another chosen by his parents for financial and social reasons. Nowadays, this hardly happens at all anymore. Even in India, the world's center of the arranged marriage, more and more young people want to marry for love.

While all this represents fantastic new freedoms for men, to be able to explore and live into all parts of himself and to feel fulfillment in a multidimensional way, it also presents significant new challenges.

Too Busy to Stop

Modern man today does not have the opportunity to come home from hunting and then sit and stare at a fire. The hundred thousand demands of work are followed by the hundred thousand demands of home. His nervous system has not rewired itself quickly enough to catch up with the dramatic change of lifestyle. He still needs space and withdrawal in order to detach from the demands of the day. In solitude, in stillness, he finds his center again.

Most of the new opportunities that a man has—to explore loving and nurturing relationships, to be a good and present father, and to participate in the home—are connecting him more with his feminine side. But this can also cause him to feel uncentered and lost in a sea of feelings. In order to remain connected with himself, a man has to be conscious not to lose touch with his masculine essence. If a man makes his whole life about merging and intimacy and does not take the time to pull away and reestablish his autonomy, he is unable to effectively deal with the stress of the day.

John says: I see in marriages that couples fall in love but lose their passion quickly because they don't create enough distance between themselves to maintain attraction. A Conscious Man is able to recognize that he has a need for intimacy, but he also has a need for solitude and silence. Particularly younger men today don't feel they have permission to acknowledge and honor their masculine side, which is autonomous and independent and wants to withdraw and take space. When he tries to take space, it can easily feel like pulling back and withdrawing his love. If the woman then tries to pursue him, he finds himself split between his desire for harmony and intimacy and his desire to connect more deeply with himself. It may appear to the woman that he has commitment issues, but it can simply mean that he is not getting enough space. To avoid becoming needy and weak, he needs to come back to a sense of fulfillment and wellbeing that is not dependent on anything outside of himself.

The way for a man to consciously create balance and to return to himself so that he can enjoy all that life has to offer to him is to know how to consciously and gracefully take space and to honor him according to the way his nervous system is wired.

Not Unisex

Both men and women need to understand that their ways of neutralizing stress are different. John says: You can see this in any movie theater. Look around, and you'll see that ninety percent of the men are sitting straight up because they are focused on the movie. At the same time, a high percentage of the women are leaning over towards their man. Men replenish themselves through being focused and alert and at the same time still. Women replenish themselves through a feeling of connection.

Men balance stress with testosterone, and women balance stress with oxytocin. You can read about this in much more detail in John's book *Why Mars and Venus Collide.*

When a woman connects with other women, without any work-related agenda or through touch and pleasure felt in the body, it releases oxytocin, the feel-good hormone that neutralizes her stress. On the other hand, when a man experiences solitude, silence, stillness, or a subjective feeling of being centered, it reduces his stress. When there is sufficient dopamine and serotonin in his brain, it allows for the replenishment of testosterone levels. This makes him feel ready to face challenges with new courage and energy.

Facing the many demands of his life depletes a man of testosterone. When he takes a break, his reserve will naturally start rebuilding, but it rebuilds faster when he is not focused on any external activity, his spine is straight, and his eyes are closed. This is sometimes known as "meditation." Light stimulates serotonin, but darkness or closed eyes allows for dopamine to increase, which is the precursor to testosterone replenishment. If you lay down, this will convert to melatonin and make you sleepy. If you sit up, the increase in dopamine will stimulate testosterone replenishment.

Although both men and women have evolved tremendously into having much greater freedom of choice, understanding these fundamental differences in the way that we each deal with stress is essential to enjoying a harmonious life.

The Urban Yogi

Whenever a man takes space, it is a movement in the direction of returning to his true nature as limitless space. That has been the quest of yogis and mystics throughout history. A man may not be conscious of his drive for the infinite, but when he comes home and seeks to forget the problems of the day, his woman might ask him, "What are you thinking?" He replies, "Nothing." These periods of blankness or emptiness, when he is not on his mission or relating to anyone, are extremely important. Boundaries drop away. It is a movement in the direction of infinite space.

For women, they experience a return to their true nature as a movement in the direction of pure love. When a woman is able to share and express her feelings without restriction, she feels more connected to a vaster, mystical, and unconditional love. Ultimately, the pursuit of infinite spaciousness is also a return to love, and the pursuit of love is also a return to infinite space.

When a man withdraws, he creates a context of space around the content of his life. Such capacity to return to the greatest space makes the challenges and problems of his life seem relatively smaller and therefore more manageable. This increases his sense of confidence and his knowing that "I can do it." Without space, he feels endlessly distracted by the latest email, the latest tweet, or the latest demand from his children or partner, and he loses connection not only with himself but also with his reason for being here at all. But when he takes space, everything falls into place and into context. He feels realigned with his purpose, and he is able to make conscious choices again.

Returning to a feeling of being spacious allows a man one of the most important qualities to being conscious and inspired: the sense of fully participating rather than winning at all costs. He finds himself able to jump in fully into his marriage, into his role as a father, into his business, and into giving all his gifts as fully as possible. This is the balance of rest and activity, of participation and withdrawal. A Conscious Man does not participate so completely that he loses connection with himself. But he does not withdraw so completely that he forgets his mission. His balance of fully giving and fully withdrawing is the key to what makes him conscious.

WHAT GETS IN THE WAY

Oftentimes, simply bringing awareness to unconscious ways of behaving allows us to relax, to return to what is natural and easy and also to that which brings the best results. So every time we examine together what gets in the way, please do not worry too much about how to get rid of it. Bringing awareness to automatic habits does not necessarily bring immediate change of behavior; but it makes you a more Conscious Man.

Detail-Oriented Desmond

The primary habit that makes it difficult for contemporary man to take the space that he needs, to return back to himself, is the sense of being overwhelmed by a never-ending torrent of small details that require urgent attention. Of course, dramatic advances in technology have made this feeling immensely stronger. Hardly a few minutes go by without a text, or an email, or a call, or the equally alluring distraction of TV, radio, tweets and Facebook updates, and... it never seems to end. Living in a hyperactive world like this can cause us, as men, to feel that there is always another fire to put out. Even when there is nothing immediate to do in front of you, it can still leave you with the continuous feeling of something mildly important that got forgotten. This makes it difficult to take space. The sense of distraction, of small details to attend to, becomes addictive. When was the last time you sat at the gate waiting to board a plane or in a doctor's waiting room? These are all opportunities to be still, to feel the environment around you, and to practice pure waiting and being aware. But today, we rarely allow ourselves to do that. Perhaps just like us, small gaps in your day easily get filled by pulling out the smart phone or lifting the lid on the laptop and filling in the few moments of "nothing to do" with finding "something to do." It's keeping busy.

It can be very uncomfortable when you finally decide to sit still. Many men say the practice of stillness is very difficult because when you do sit still and even close your eyes, the rapid movement of attention from one thing to another keeps going, even in the absence of any external stimulus. The key here is not to try and make the mind quiet and still but simply to notice with curiosity, and sometimes even with amazement, how wildly the machine is spinning out of control. Simply making this amused recognition will not immediately change your state, but it will return attention to something deeper, something that is conscious and aware and present even in the midst of rapid mental activity. That is pure awareness, and that is the deeper dimension of you calling yourself home.

Obligation Oliver

Much more than in any previous generation, men today aspire to being fully involved in family life. We want to be loving and caring partners. We want to be good fathers. We have felt what it is like to be present and involved. We like it. This aspiration to be a good man, not only in our own eyes but also in the eyes of other people, creates a relational pull: a feeling of obligation to participate. And so, retreating into solitude or "cave time" can easily feel like self-indulgence or like you are denying other people what they rightly deserve from you.

Many men say that this kind of pull becomes particularly strong when they come home at the end of the workday. A man might tell us his honest truth: he wants some time to withdraw. He has had it with the demands of other people and with the swirling, churning confusion of the world. But as he opens the door, he is greeted by his partner and the excited bright-eyed demands of his children. Now he faces a whole new set of obligations. His partner has also been working all day. Now, caring for children, preparing food, and supervising homework, is part of his duty. The thought of taking 20 or 30 minutes to withdraw from everything and find his center again causes him to feel guilty. Some men turn to alcohol or marijuana or even to other substances to dampen down this feeling of wanting to explode.

Confused Charlie

For a man who lives together with a woman, he may face the challenge that she does not empathize with his desire for solitude and withdrawal. Women recover from stress through connecting and bonding, talking, and listening. This does not work for a man in the same way: he has a capacity to simply make problems go away quite quickly when he closes the door on them.

Consequently, a man often feels that when he is overwhelmed and needs to find center, his woman will want to support him by encouraging him to sit down and talk about it. When he says to his wife, "I need some time to be quiet and take a break now," her response is, "That's a good idea honey, let's go sit on the back porch together and talk about what's going on." Unless a man becomes deeply conscious of what works for him and what works in a different way for her, he may become confused and wonder why what works for her is not working for him. A woman will quickly conclude that a man is depressed if he wants to withdraw or that he no longer loves her. He may even end up believing her.

Wound-Up Walter

A man today faces life and death challenges: emergencies that require immediate attention... all the while sitting in an office chair, staring at a screen. His body is releasing stress hormones, the instinct to enter into battle or to run away fast, but he is not moving at all. His body is not getting physically tired, and so it is not sending the necessary messages to stop and rest. He is low on the dopamine that helps him focus but gets no trigger to replenish himself. He is all wound up. Unable to relax, his busy brain shifts this nervous energy from focusing on the things that really need to get done to watching YouTube videos, playing video games, or just aimlessly cruising the Web.

A great solution is to consciously create artificial ways to physically exhaust yourself either as a break during the middle of the day or when you finish work. Going to a gym or running will give your body the feeling that it has worked hard and now deserves a break as much as your mind does. After a good workout, it is much easier to be still and quiet.

THE PRACTICES

Somehow or other, it is important to make stillness and withdrawal from the world an equally high priority as being on your mission, getting your work done, and being present for your family. One helpful key is to expand your ideas of what taking a break should look like.

As we already discussed, the more that you need a period of withdrawal and stillness, the more difficult it may be for you to give that to yourself. The more wound up you are, the more the thoughts are flying randomly in different directions, the more your body is running on adrenalin and cortisol, and the more uncomfortable sitting still will feel to you. The key is to make taking space all about watching and being aware of what is happening in your body and mind. Forget your ambitions to be silent and still and peaceful.

Body Scan

A good way to practice this is to sit still for 15 to 20 minutes and simply to scan your body. It is a great idea to sit into the back of the chair and then to have your spine upright and straight. Try not to slouch. When the spine is straight, it allows the spinal fluid to flow easily between the base of the spine and the skull. When your spine is erect and straight in this way, you will fall more quickly into a feeling of being centered and present, and the world will more quickly drop away.

It is also a great idea to be aware of how deeply you are breathing. At the beginning, it is simply that. You must be aware of the way that it already is. But awareness of how you are breathing will also gradually allow your breath to become deeper. The more that your belly is moving with each breath, the more quickly you will experience stress melting away and the return to a feeling of wellbeing that has no external cause.

Now you can simply be aware of different sensations in the body. Notice the soles of your feet. Notice the muscles in your calves and then in your thighs. Become aware of the sensations in your belly, and take some time to notice each organ. Notice the sensations in the lower back and in the middle part of the back up into the shoulders. You can notice the feelings in your chest, your throat, and your face. A scan like this, simply noticing what is going on in the body, will amplify the quality of awareness. After 15 to 20 minutes, you will feel more connected with being aware and being awareness itself than with simply being a body.

Physical Ways to Take Space

When sitting quietly feels uncomfortable, or even impossible, cut yourself some slack. Try more physical ways to practice conscious withdrawal. We both enjoy walking. In fact, we created this entire book by taking walks together in the beautiful countryside of Marin County. Walking can be just as effective a way of connecting with yourself as sitting. In the same way, practicing yoga, Chi Kung, martial arts, or any other form of physical activity that causes you to feel more centered and present could be great ways to take space and come back to yourself. Fishing, golf, or hiking may also give you the opportunity you need to withdraw and come back to feeling free within yourself.

Relax Your Censorship on Practice

Many men develop unnecessary, rigid ideas about what constitutes daily practice. For example, here is a practice that has proven to be immensely helpful to some men and in fact has become a rocket ship to the peaks of nirvana. It is an ancient spiritual practice that has been handed down through thousands of years, dating back to sacred texts in Tibet.

Here is how to do it:

1. Go into a room alone.
2. You will need some very specific ritual equipment for this practice to be effective. You will need to buy a very comfortable chair. The La-Z-Boy and Stressless brands can probably help you out. You will also need a television and a remote control.
3. Now recline fully in the chair, and adjust your television to transmit images of other men performing heroic acts of physical prowess. Football, basketball, and baseball are very effective examples.

Watching a game in this way may be the most powerful and effective form of meditation for you. Be aware and curious about what activities genuinely neutralize stress in a way that allows you to return to the demands of your family and the world with something to give.

Take a Day to Unplug

Once a week, it is an invaluable idea to take a day where you do not have to accomplish anything. Of course, some of this day will be spent with your family where your focus will be primarily on their needs. But a day to unplug like this should also include some time to be by yourself. Many men have an area of the house or even somewhere away from the house where they can tinker with things that appear to be vaguely useful.

Arjuna says: I have a shed on our property that is theoretically my woodwork shop. I go to my shop and organize screws into different lengths and then put them into neat little containers. I repair things often that were not being used in the first place anyway. It's all an excuse; it's a place where I can go to be by myself and do things that are not urgent. No one else in my family has the slightest interest in joining me there. I've created a place where I can withdraw with some vague appearance of doing something useful, and I can recharge myself. It's really great to find your own equivalent to my woodwork shop. Have a place where you can go and be by yourself and you know you can be left alone until you're ready to come out and play again.

The Full Monty

Once or twice a year, try to get away from it all. We already talked about this in the previous chapter about mission and purpose. You can find the specific suggestions we have there for a five-day retreat. Some men like to take a motorcycle trip or go sailing for a few days or on a camping trip. It is completely different to do this with your partner or with your family than it is to do this by yourself or with other men. Family vacations are great, the stuff of great memories that will last you for the rest of your life. But they do not necessarily allow you to be washed clean of the hundred thousand distractions of day-to-day life. Do whatever you can to create space for yourself for a few days, and you will come back to the world again with a whole new wave of something original and glorious to offer.

Communicate It

Being able to explain your need for space and withdrawal to other people, especially if you are in relationship with a woman, is a rarefied art form. Remember, because she knows how to revitalize herself through agenda-free relating, particularly with other women, most women will not understand the need for withdrawal and solitude and may interpret it as a sign that you are depressed and that you need nurturing.

So the first step is for you to get clear with yourself when you actually need time to be alone and to put the rest of the world at a distance.

The second step is to become clear, in a scientific and measurable way, about the effect that taking space has for you when you come out again. Find ways to take space that really do allow you to have something greater to give. It has got to work. You can try meditation, running, fishing, hiking, walking, tinkering, Chi Kung, yoga... You've got to find the key that fits your personal lock. Once you find it and you know that it works, you have something that you can communicate with confidence.

The third step is to be able to explain your need to take space and withdraw in the context of having more to give. But you cannot fake it. You have got to know for real that if you take space, everyone will benefit. So now, you can come home from work and you can say something like this to your partner and to your children or to anyone else who may seem like they need something from you:

> *"I love you. I don't just want to show up when I'm feeling brain dead and exhausted. I need about half an hour of alone time, no more than that. Then my batteries will be recharged, and I can be with you in the way that I want to be with you and in the way that you deserve."*

Obviously, you do not want to read this aloud as a script. Your partner will just end up saying to you, "You sound like John Gray and Arjuna Ardagh right now." Dig into the gist of what we are saying here, and you will find a way to contextualize the idea of taking space for the people you live with so that it feels like a gift instead of taking something away.

FOR WOMEN

A man who takes space regularly will generally be able to be more fully present with you and with everyone else as well. We all get stressed in today's world, but men and women release stress in different ways, and we all tend to forget that. Most women (but not all) regenerate themselves by being relational, especially with other women. A famous study done at UCLA showed that when women get together just to share lunch, so long as they are not talking about work-related things, oxytocin levels double within an hour. It is not like that for men. For thousands of years, men have balanced the testosterone-driven activities of the day with periods of stillness, silence, and withdrawal. Even within 20 to 30 minutes, increased levels of dopamine cause testosterone reserves to replenish, and then a man has something to give to the world again — something to give to you.

It can be very difficult for both men and women to understand this difference in biology. The huge advances in social equality we have seen in the last decades have caused many people to want to discount biological differences between men and women because they can appear sexist or seem to encourage stereotyping. But ignoring these differences can also cause misunderstanding in intimate relationships.

If you are married or you live with a man, it may be difficult for him to even recognize that he needs space and withdrawal. Some men even feel guilty: it may seem like a symptom of not wanting to participate fully in family life. But if he finds the right way to regenerate, he will have so much more to give once he comes out from his cave. Cave time might range from a traditional meditation practice to just reclining in a favorite chair and watching a game on the TV for a little while.

If you want a happy man in your life, a man who can be fully present with you, a man who can make love with you and be totally present, please find a way to see his periods of withdrawal time as a fundamentally important preparation for being able to show up with you in the way that you long for.

Do not try to share cave time with him. When you can see him starting to withdraw, let him go. You may feel that you want to give him a shoulder to cry on or offer an ear to talk to. But this does not work in the same way that it works for a woman. Men come back to themselves more by forgetting about problems for a while rather than by talking them through. When he wants to take a walk or go sit on the back deck or just slink away somewhere, recognize that this is part of his cycle of tapping back in to the source of all that he has to give to you.

Some women interpret periods of withdrawal and solitude as taking love away. It is his way of being able to restore balance, so he has more love to give. Everyone has feelings of abandonment sometimes. If that happens for you, share with him how you feel, and then still let him go. If a man feels that it is not okay with you for him to withdraw, he may easily shut that impulse down. There are so many ways to mess up as a man, to not get it right, and men are just as sensitive to criticism as women. But then it is to everyone's detriment. An uncentered, distracted, stressed-out man has absolutely nothing to give to anybody.

If he takes periods of space and then still seems moody and withdrawn, there may be a deeper problem. His ways of taking space may not be working for him. He may be genuinely depressed. He may have lost his sense of mission and purpose and may feel useless and without any value. These are real feelings that all men have sometimes. His way of recovering from that will be different from what feels intuitive to you. Remind him to take a break from it all. If he can feel that it is really okay with you to go camping alone for a few days or to go on a road trip with his buddies and that there will be no negative consequences, that may be the fastest way for him to get out of a funk: faster perhaps than therapy or talking about problems.

If you are single and ready to welcome a Conscious Man into your life to share love with you, a man who regularly takes space will almost certainly be a man who has more to give to you, and he will be able to receive your love more fully. A man who has a daily meditation practice, or any other kind of structured and disciplined way to withdraw regularly from the world, will generally make a better partner and a better husband and can be more attentive to your needs. He can meet you in a much deeper and more genuine way: in the way that you may be longing for in your heart of hearts.

A Conscious Man:

MEET KUTE BLACKSON, FOUNDER OF LOVE NOW

bout fourteen years ago when I was twenty-three, I remember
driving one afternoon from Los Angeles to San Diego. I was
frustrated, broke, and unhappy in my relationship with my
girlfriend. I felt stuck and was tired of reading self-help books for answers—I
had read six or seven hundred and still hadn't found the answers I needed. I
drove down the 405 screaming, "God, I'm so frustrated! Aaaahhh, my life!
I wanna know God, I want to know him."

That was when I heard a voice say, "Walk the Camino…." The Camino
de Santiago, as in the pilgrimage in Spain. But I didn't have the money for
the trip and had a host of other excuses why the journey was not practical.
A few days later I met my best friend and told him about the voice I had
heard urging me to walk the Camino, and he promptly wrote me a check
for ten thousand dollars.

So I flew to Spain. I shaved my head, packed a backpack with two
sets of clothes, and had no idea what I was doing. The first day I walked
eighteen kilometers in the Pyrenees. I was immersed in a complete fog,
unable to see farther than a foot in front of me. I was so scared and cried
those first few days, wondering, "What am I doing?" and thinking, "I am
going to die."

Everything rose up in my mind for me to see: the fears, the insanity,
the craziness, the judgments. It was all going non-stop and was very

challenging. Many times I thought I wasn't going to make it. I cried and screamed; I prayed and I questioned God.

Despite the challenges, I pressed on and found a way of walking the Camino. I learned that no matter what, I had to love myself along the journey. I was silent for most of the walk. I made peace with myself and with my past. I learned to trust life in a way I had never trusted before.

I surrendered everything when I went into this pilgrimage. I gave up the need to have a purpose, the need to make a difference, and the need to be different. I gave up all of my dreams, too—like my dream to write a book. I just gave it all up and said, "God... I give up every ambition, and if that means I become the street sweeper, then that's my destiny." When I got back to Los Angeles, I didn't do much for several months. I just sat there. I broke up with my girlfriend. I went to a couple of parties and I felt awkward. I'd just sit there and think, "How do I speak to people? How do I speak to this girl?"

A few months later something started to shift. It was not the old sense of "Let me go and do this thing," but rather an emerging. My hand was reaching out for the phone. It felt very subtle, very different, like something was moving me to make the call. It was a very distinct moment, a sense of being moved.

I felt such freedom, such peacefulness, and so in love with everything. I wanted other people to experience this sensation, too, so I got my first coaching client. The man was on drugs and I took him through a process of unraveling and healing, peeling the layers away and connecting him with his essence. His life changed within a month, completely and radically. And he told everybody. One by one, new clients showed up, and their lives changed radically, too. And the work just kept growing.

Now there is a lot of action in my life, at least on the surface. I don't think I'd be able to be present and remain calm and free in the world if I had not accessed that deep foundation on the Camino. I still have to unplug on a daily basis. I take time to go inside. I believe in the importance of taking space, accessing that spaciousness, and then coming back into the world from that foundation.

Chapter Three

HE KNOWS HOW TO LOVE DEEPLY

A Conscious Man has learned to ask himself two centrally important questions. When he asks, "Who am I?" he withdraws from the world to discover who he is on his own terms. When he asks, "Why am I here?" he sets back out into the world to discover what he has to give. The balance of these two creates a context of dignity and purpose. Now you are no longer out just to get something for yourself. You are developing a generous relationship to life where you are overflowing with something you want to give. Instead of being a consumer, you are becoming a contributor.

When we have lost our way, it is much too difficult to love. Then we feel afraid, we take ourselves so seriously, and there is too much on the line. It requires a certain rootedness in yourself for it to be safe to open your heart.

Sitting on a meditation cushion is safe. When you are working in a company or serving clients, there is also not so much vulnerability at stake. Learning to love in a more personal way requires greater courage. When you learn to set things right with everyone close to you so they all feel deeply loved, your bigger mission is more likely to be infused with real presence and authenticity.

Personal, intimate love brings integration and completion both to your sense of mission and to your periods of inner withdrawal. The courage to love makes them both more real and powerful. It is where you have the greatest possibility for real development as a man.

We are all growing out of the old kind of relationship that was based in a tacit agreement of exchange. A man used to think, *OK, so now I am providing for her; I give her a home, financial security, and food. It is her duty to have sex with me and to raise my children. She owes me.* A Conscious Man does not go to a woman to fill himself up; he goes to share what he already has. It is the shift from caring about success to caring about someone he can share his success with that creates a depth of love.

Relationship Aikido

When your partner does not have so much to give, it is easy to feel resentful, and this can sabotage the relationship. When we learn to let go of that, her occasional judgments and reactions to you are no longer like a wind that blows the tree over. You are grounded. You have developed deep roots in your sense of purpose and in knowing who you are in a deeper way than fleeting thoughts and feelings. You are no longer dependent upon your partner's affection and approval and acceptance to define you as a man. You are able to love deeply exactly because you are able to define yourself independently of the relationship.

Relationship becomes an opportunity to dig even deeper into yourself, to give more, and to become a stronger and deeper man. Instead of waiting for her to change, it is an opportunity to make a change within yourself, come back to an unconditionally loving place, and give more to the relationship. When you feel under attack, you can ask yourself, "What is going on inside me? What can I do to build a bridge with her again?"

You are not dependent upon a relationship to know yourself, but you are dependent upon being in a relationship to grow in that self-knowledge. When you have children, it goes to even another level of maturity. Now you are extending beyond the reciprocity of a romantic relationship to the unconditional giving of being a parent. Your children owe you nothing. The greatest growth for both of us has been in being a father: to be able to give to our children without any expectation that our happiness is dependent upon them.

Slowly, we learn to give up the feeling of being a victim in the relationship because ultimately, a Conscious Man is in a process of learning to be accountable for everything in his life. You can learn every day to let go of the past and develop the capacity to create your own future. You can take responsibility for creating the relationship that you want by bringing out the best in your partner just as she can learn to bring out the best in you.

This requires us to be grounded in conscious masculinity, but it also calls for tools and skills, many of which we did not learn from our families and childhood.

Love Is a Practice

John says: I remember a moment seven years into my marriage. After making love with Bonnie, I said to her, "That was fantastic. It was as good as it was in the beginning."

"Oh, I thought it was much better," she replied.

"Really? How so?" I asked her.

"In the beginning we had great sex," she said, "but we didn't really know each other then. Now you've seen the best of me, and you've seen the worst of me, and you still adore me." When she said that, I had to stop and think. I had never thought of it that way. It was a moment of becoming more conscious as a man. The love we had built in seven years had made the sex much more fulfilling.

To love deeply is to experience all of who a person is. It's not to fantasize that she is perfect but to grow and love someone who is not perfect simply because you have made a decision to love more each day. You create friendships in life by giving; they do not just happen automatically. Equally, you can create a great marriage. It starts with a fantasy, and you create it through give-and-take. In those times when it is difficult to give and your partner needs you, you rise to the occasion. You made a promise to your partner. There are temptations and distractions, and you rise above them because you made a commitment. You grow in love.

Ultimately, your relationship becomes sacred. The words "sacred" and "sacrifice" both come from the same Latin root, "sacer," which means holy. When you make sacrifices for someone, you make that person special. You make it a sacred relationship.

We have all had the experience of falling in love, which usually happens when we first meet someone we do not yet know very well. It is a glimpse of seeing just how beautiful everything can be when you truly open your eyes and your heart. But it is not yet grounded. You need practice to ground it, to stabilize it, to integrate it, and to live it.

One of the greatest obstacles that men face is the expectation that love should be automatic, just as it was in the beginning when there was nothing you had to do. That glimpse was the result of chemistry and bumping into the right person at the right time. However, that particular configuration of forces will quickly disappear, and then you have to commit yourself to the practice of opening up that portal again and again and again. It is tempting to assume that it is your right to experience those feelings, and when they go away, it must be your partner's fault. Then we get frustrated because we have the unrealistic expectation that romance, affection, attraction, and passion should be automatic if you are with the right person.

Remember with Netflix, or one hundred thousand other things available on the Internet, that you can get the first month free? They are hoping you get hooked. Then you have to pay. It is just like that with the practice of love. You get a free glimpse when you fall in love, and then you need to be prepared to make regular payments through daily practice.

Learning to love is best measured not by how you feel inside yourself but by how other people feel in your presence. It is relatively easy to be impressed with your own state of maturity. When you get to the point that your partner, or your teenage children, are impressed by your love, then and only then will you know that you are onto something. It requires your making your life into an art form instead of an accident.

You discover that love is not just a feeling that comes over you sometimes. It's something you can choose, it's something you can practice, it's something you can develop, and it's something that you can become.

Transcend Your Genetics

Through practice, you learn to move beyond your genetics and your conditioning, and you begin to transform your ability to love as a deliberate art form.

We can understand this better by thinking about your body. You might have been born to muscular, stocky parents. Then you are naturally a solid and muscular guy. You do not have to do anything. You might equally have been born to tall, skinny parents, so you resemble something like a stick insect. ("Just like me," says Arjuna.) If you just eat and sleep and go about your day, you will probably end up looking like a blended version of your parents and your grandparents.

Some men choose to put energy into sculpting their bodies into a consciously chosen work of art. Arjuna says: My oldest son, Abhi, is a great example. In his teen years, he looked just like me. When he started to spurt up, he had matchstick legs, just like mine. But at some point he said, "I don't think I want to just have the body I was born with through genetics. I think I'd like to craft my own." At 16, he started to go to the gym. He worked out religiously. He has also learned a tremendous amount about nutrition. He has studied how to do weightlifting consciously so that he does not damage his body. Now he weighs about 190 pounds instead of the 150 pounds he would have weighed otherwise. When he shows up in a room, his physical presence is not determined just by the hand he was dealt. It's the result of conscious choice and skill and discipline. You are seeing his commitment to creating something consciously chosen.

Whether you are born with positive conditioning or negative conditioning, it still leads to unconscious behavior. You might have been born into an incredibly dysfunctional family, where your parents were fighting, drinking, or even being violent. You might have grown up and started to duplicate some of those same habits. Then you might have had the terrifying thought that you are turning into your parents. Or you might have been born into a loving, beautiful, harmonious household, where Mom and Dad were kissing and cuddling and saying, "Honey." You might have grown up to marry your high school sweetheart and to live the same life.

Those are two kinds of conditioning. One looks pretty; one looks ugly. But living out either of one of them, as a genetic inevitability, would be equally unconscious. Conscious masculinity means that you learn to love as a deliberate practice.

In this sense, an unhappy childhood gives you an advantage because this makes it really obvious that you need to learn the practice of love. When everything was rosy most of the time, you may have grown up with what we call "unconscious competence." It means that you have the perfect training to create a positive relationship if we were still living in the same environment that existed thirty years ago. But we are in a constantly changing and new world. The traditional roles may have taken thousands and thousands of years to develop, but most of them do not work anymore.

So whether you were born into a very functional family or born into a very dysfunctional family, both can be formulas for disaster unless you become conscious of your masculinity and recognize that every day is a choice to practice the art of love.

Presence Is the Key

It all comes down to being present. Everyone in your life is craving, more than anything, for you to show up with all of you in your body and be present. That is what really gives nourishment.

Arjuna says: Sometimes I walk into the room, and Chameli is disturbed by something. She might say, "The place is such a mess." My unconscious habit is to start frantically running around the room cleaning things up to try and get her approval. I've learned that the first thing to do is to drop more deeply into my body and to come back feeling connected with myself. It is only possible to do that if I have a daily practice of taking space and withdrawing. Then, I can look right into her eyes, I can smile, and I can let that smile come all the way from my lower belly. I can say, "I am definitely going to clean up this mess," but those words are just floating on the surface. Right under the surface is a wave of presence looking right into her and saying, in an unspoken way, "I'm right here. Feel me. I've got this. You can relax."

That is the key. You do not always need to say those words out loud but just convey their meaning through your body. That is the greatest gift that a man can give to a woman.

When She Earns More Money

We both often hear from men who are married to women who make more money than they do. This can stir up all of the ideas about what it means to be a good man. Just a couple of generations ago, this was primarily measured by his capacity to provide for her physically: money, security, food, and warmth.

We both have very different experiences of this. In John's case, he is the primary income provider in the family. Bonnie works part time in the office and also takes care of the home and the vegetable garden and cooks fantastic food. On the other hand, Chameli makes more money than Arjuna does: she is a very successful international teacher. But despite very different economic circumstances, John and I find that we have the same experience of what it takes to love a woman deeply.

When a woman makes more money than her partner, it could be an opportunity for the man to go more into his feminine side and then possibly to lose his sense of mission. It can also become a great opportunity for a man to grow even more rooted in his true gift. This is not measured so much in terms of whether he makes more or less money but depends on if he is really living in his purpose. Chameli has no problem with making more money if she knows that Arjuna is doing what he was born to do on the planet.

Arjuna says: I coached a couple in their early 30s. They both had good jobs, but he wanted to quit his job and write the book that he could feel was begging to push its head down the creative "birth canal." He didn't have a big advance from his publisher, but the shifts in our social fabric caused him to earn no money for a year while his wife supported them both. He still felt rooted in his self-confidence, and she still felt proud of him that she could trust him more. This was possible because he had considered giving his gift as a higher priority over merely financial goals.

WHAT GETS IN THE WAY

Impatient Isaac

When you go to the gym to build muscle, you will not get very far by sticking with the 5 and 10 pound weights. You need to crank it up to the point that you feel a challenge to complete your set. That is when you see progress. Learning to love also requires you to be willing to face challenges. There will be times when a woman may appear to make things difficult for you. When she feels ignored or neglected, it may sometimes seem impossible to figure out what is going on for her, and it may seem impossible to make her happy.

The greatest challenge for a man to learn to love deeply is to understand that her nervous system is wired quite differently. She gets stressed by going to work often in environments that were created by men. She faces many of the same challenges that we do, but pushing through and meeting deadlines does not give her the same buzz as it gives us. She is solving problems all day, but it may not work for her to withdraw to a cave and forget about the world.

When she has a nurturing partner who is present, who is attentive, who plans dates and shows affection, and who listens carefully and gives reassuring comments, this stimulates oxytocin and lowers her stress.

Here is the crash course of what we know: all actions of love are equal to all other actions of love for a woman, and she needs frequent and repeated expressions of love. You could buy her 36 beautiful red roses once a week, and you will give her a huge surge of oxytocin. You can also give her one rose, and it will create the same surge. Keep giving her that one rose again and again, and you can continue to give her the same surge of oxytocin, over and over again. Stress will diminish, her heart will open, and she will feel loved by you.

Forgetful Freddy

Arjuna says: Years ago, I was in an antique shop in England. Tucked away on a high shelf there was a metal plate that had been removed from the side of an agricultural machine. The sign said, "Do not attempt to put machine in gear until operator is present." I bought it. I kept it with me for decades from one house to another. It became my mantra. It is a great maxim to remember in learning to love deeply.

We forget the power of presence. You can come home, give your wife a peck on the cheek, and mumble the perfunctory, "I love you." But if she cannot feel that you are fully present, it means nothing. In the same way, you could come home, look at her deeply in the eyes, sink into your body a little bit so you can feel your feet on the earth, look not at her but deeply into her eyes, and then say, "I forgot to buy the butter." If she can feel you deeply with her, fully present, the second way of meeting will touch her much more than the first. She will swoon.

Wounded Willy

One of the greatest obstacles to growing deeply in love is that sensitivities take over. When you are dancing very close to someone, there is more of a chance that this person might step on your foot. We are all to some degree still influenced by relationships we had in childhood, particularly with our mothers. You cannot make the past go away. But if it is unconscious or not acknowledged, it is going to run everything. When old wounds from the past come to the surface, they do not come with a large neon label that says "Warning: This is an unresolved issue with your mother." Instead, you find yourself becoming judgmental and critical and blaming someone. You may even feel threatened and get defensive and feel she is accusing you of something. We will explore how to deal with these wounds in the next chapter.

Dogmatic Douglas

The old hyper-masculine trance, out of which we are evolving, was very much identified with being right. The patriarch of the family could not be questioned. He knew what was correct and incorrect, and only he knew what was factual and what was fiction. Although our way of life has changed a great deal, we all know that the shadow of these habits still remains. The key is not so much to get rid of it, but to tell the truth to yourself and everybody else that it is there. We need to be aware of when we choose the shallow victory of winning an argument over the deeper satisfaction of sharing love.

Fuzzy Phillipe

There are so many more ways to have an intimate relationship today than just the old model of suburban family life. You can choose to be single, celibate, monogamous, or polyamorous, to name just a few of the fantastic possibilities. There are all kinds of ways to explore your sexuality, but in order to love deeply, it is important to make clear agreements and to keep to them.

As a man, you probably notice beautiful women all day long. It is part of our nature to be constantly on the lookout for new opportunities and challenges. Noticing a beautiful woman, and noticing that she is noticing you, can lift your energy and brighten your day no matter what your circumstances.

Just for the record, after being in marriages of 30 and 13 years each, we have both found that staying with the same woman, loving her more and more deeply each day, and deepening the commitment every day, opens a depth of beauty in each of our wives that we have never known through other relationships that were less committed. We have found that monogamy takes you to depths of love that for us cannot be reached in any other way.

Sometimes, loving very deeply may require sacrificing more immediate and enticing pleasures. It may mean staying present in situations where you feel uncomfortable when you want to run away. A significant obstacle to loving deeply is to follow what feels good at the moment but in that way selling out something more sustained.

THE PRACTICES

Bring the Gift of Presence

When you walk into a room, get into the habit of remembering your lower belly before you speak.

Take a deep breath, deep enough that it pushes your lower belly out a bit. You might even put your hand there for a moment to remember. Count slowly from 1 to 3.

Make eye contact before you say anything. Have a sense of not looking at your partner, but into your partner, almost like you are playing "peek-a-boo" with the deepest part of her.

Give the gift of cool, calm, collected presence. If you don't feel cool, calm, and collected, it may be time to withdraw just for a few minutes to drop into your center more deeply. A few minutes of practicing Chi Kung or another physical exercise can really help.

Let your presence communicate the sense of "I'm right here," so she can feel it clearly whether you say it or not. Sometimes it helps to take a very small step forward towards your partner as she is telling you what she is feeling.

Pure Listening

We have a whole chapter coming up about listening. It is a pivotal key to loving in a way that can be received. Because men are identified with action and accomplishment, they think that providing a solution is the most tangible measurement of love. But remember: she releases oxytocin when she can speak freely about her feelings without necessarily needing a solution.

The key is to listen, ask questions, be curious, and go easy on the solutions.

Deepen Trust and Monogamy

We already talked about the challenges men face by feeling attracted in many directions. If you are a man who—like us—chooses monogamy, the most important key is a level of honesty that is so moment to moment and so detail oriented that things never build up and become a big deal.

Arjuna says: I tell my wife about small attractions that I feel throughout my day. Even if I have a dream that features a beautiful woman, I might tell Chameli about the dream in the morning. If you practice this kind of meticulous honesty on a day-to-day basis, it may not be entirely comfortable, especially at the beginning, but it will build trust in a way that you might not expect. She knows that you are healthy normal man, who experiences sexual energy, but you also have the presence to feel it and not act on it.

Feel this energy fully when it comes to you. Enjoy it as a pleasurable feeling in your body, as a rush of aliveness, as an opening of your heart. Be grateful that you are having this feeling of pleasurable energy.

Direct this feeling, once it is alive in you, back to thinking about your partner. Perhaps you are having dinner with a beautiful woman when you are out of town for business or any other reason. If you notice a flush of attraction, feel it fully, and then tell her about how much you love your wife.

Or if you are traveling and not going straight home to your partner, write her a romantic letter, or call her up, and bring these feelings of arousal back to remembering your attraction for her. These conscious practices train your mind and body to sustain romantic feelings for your body.

Re-create Polarization

Many couples feel challenged by the ways that we share so many of the same tasks. We both go to work, we both go buy groceries, we both pick up the kids, we both cook food, and in fact, we both do all the same things. Because our roles merge so much, it is easy for the polarization of masculine and feminine energy to get diminished, and then you feel less attraction for your partner. In this manner, you can end up feeling the love that you might feel for a friend, but the romance goes out of it.

There are some great ways to reestablish polarization. One is to spend time alone or with your men friends. If your partner spends time with women friends, you will come back together feeling more different from each other but also more attracted to each other.

Another practice that can be a lot of fun, and can quickly restore the feeling of romance and polarization, is a few hours of role-play. Arjuna says: I often coach couples in this way. I suggest that, independently from each other, they dress up in the kind of clothes they would never usually wear. For a sloppy hippie kind of guy, I would suggest he wear a very sharp black suit. For a business guy, I would suggest that he dress like a rock star. I make similar suggestions to the woman: to dress completely differently than she usually does. Then, at the appointed time, she goes to a bar or restaurant and sits alone. She has chosen a new name and a new life story for herself. A few minutes later, he arrives at the same location, walks over, and asks her if he may join her. Then they can begin to experience each other in a new light. Newness rekindles passionate feelings. It is a good idea to have a hotel room reserved because things are going to get pretty hot. Love gets shut down by taking each other for granted. The vast and unexplored mystery of the crazy firework display of possibilities contained within your partner can get shut down into the bland label of "my wife, my woman." You can reignite love by consciously getting to know each other with fresh eyes and fresh stories. The same applies to visiting new and different places together on romantic getaways.

Practice Appreciation

Appreciate the qualities that you love about your partner many times a day. Never for a moment think that you can overestimate how many times you can tell her that she looks beautiful. It never gets boring to her. You could tell your partner that she looks great at 9 o'clock in the morning, and by 11 a.m., it will be completely forgotten. You could tell her again, and it would be like saying it for the first time.

The practice of appreciation does not appeal so much to our logical, linear minds because it is not obviously useful. If something is wrong and needs fixing, that seems like useful communication. If your partner is doing something that annoys you, then asking for a change seems useful. But talking about what you already like and what feels good does not feel so useful to our problem-solving mind. Yet it makes all the difference in the world.

Try this for a month. Tell your partner five times a day something you appreciate about her.

> *Your hair looks so beautiful.*
> *I love the huge difference you make to people in your work.*
> *I appreciate that you are so creative.*
> *I love it how kind you are with people you hardly know.*
> *I love it that you cook so well.*
> *I love how you smell.*
> *You did such a great job redecorating the spare room.*

Just keep it going, hour after hour, day after day, week after week, and you will see that appreciation is the most powerful way to turn boredom and drudgery back into romance and sparkle.

A Ritual of Devotion

Human beings have always had a devotional streak. That is why there are cathedrals all over the world, mosques and temples, and endless deities and statues. However sophisticated and well educated we may think we are, there is a part of us that likes to bow down and express devotion to something vaster than what our small minds can understand.

For sure, you can bow down to a statue or a painting or to your particular idea of what "the divine" is. But you could also direct those feelings, at least in part, to your partner. Sounds strange? For most people it is. This may not be everyone's cup of tea, and you will have to see if it fits for you. But it can have spectacular results.

Arjuna says: Chameli and I have been practicing in this way for years and years, and it is probably the most powerful thing that we do together. It is very simple. In the morning, after you wake up but before you get dressed, sit opposite each other on the bed. You can also use two chairs if it feels more comfortable.

Take turns to do this simple practice. One of you can speak for only about two minutes. It can be simple statements of gratitude, appreciation and commitment, or it could even be over-the-top expressions of surrender and devotion. If you have trouble finding the right words, you could use this as a script to get you started. Feel free to use any of the following phrases I have used with Chameli.

> *I love you. I see you. You can see me more deeply than I can see myself. I surrender to your wisdom, to your clarity. Please demand the best of me today. I surrender to the wisdom of our union, to the wisdom of love itself. I feel so grateful that we can be in this journey together. Thank you so much for being here with me. Thank you so much for all the fun we have, everything we create together. If I have ever taken*

you for granted, I am sorry. And I commit to be completely honest with you. I commit to be with you. I commit to this relationship as my teacher. I love you.

Finally, you just bow down to your partner, and she can touch you lightly on your head as a kind of a blessing. If all this sounds a little "out there," imagine how good it is going to feel when you switch roles and she says all these things to you.

Then you can switch over. Your partner can bow down to you in the same way and say similar things.

This practice starts every day in a spirit of deep love. When devotion flows both ways, it can be a fantastic key to taking love to new depths.

FOR WOMEN

Men sometimes tell us they do not know how to express love to a woman in a way that means something to her. Men get very easily hung up on the feeling of succeeding or failing and can feel unsuccessful in giving love in a way that can be received.

So let him know when he is succeeding in taking some small steps towards touching your heart and when you feel loved. When you let him know that his love has affected you, it motivates him to go deeper. He thrives on a sense of "mission accomplished."

It is easy for a man to feel that he cannot succeed in making a woman happy and then easily lose his spirits. If he gives you compliments, buys you gifts, leaves little notes, or does his best to organize something to please you, make sure that you can take it in, and let yourself swoon a little. It makes a huge difference when he knows that his experiments with small gestures have hit the mark and he has had a small triumph.

Make Clear Requests

Men say that they often feel they hear a lot about what they are doing wrong and then get confused about what action or measurable change would make a difference. For example, if you come home and the kitchen is a mess or a diaper has not been changed or shopping has not been done, a Conscious Man will want to put it straight.

Do not clean up his messes for him; it is discouraging for him and causes a man to feel shame. Try to make your requests as clear and straightforward as possible. One example would be, "I want to make a nice dinner, and I forgot a cauliflower. Can you go to the store and buy one for me?" A good man loves to be able to say, "I'm right on it. I got this."

Most men thrive on accomplishing things. If you can give him specific tasks that will make a difference to you, where it is possible for him to succeed, you will get your needs met, and he will feel good about himself and inspired to love you more through actions that are meaningful to you.

Release Him from Responsibility for Your Happiness

The old habits that we are all growing out of together, as men and women, is that we can make each other happy. It is just not true.

When you are already happy, a man can make you happier. He can do little things to tickle and stimulate happiness when it is already there in you. When you are unhappy, he can be present, he can listen, and he can empathize.

A big key to supporting a man to live his full potential is to recognize that happiness is an inside job. Once you take responsibility for feeling good on your own, then a man can take you from happy to happier, just as you can do the same for him.

Make a list of all the factors in your life that you have control over and that make you unhappy. And then make another list of all the other things that you do have control over and that make you happier. For many women, such a list would include spending downtime with girlfriends, being able to relax and enjoy delicious food, enjoying scented baths, using nice oils, having beautiful clothes, and taking in fine environments.

To bring out the best in a man, do less for him, and do more to make yourself happy. John says: This is the central theme of my book Mars and Venus Collide. If you stop over-giving to men and give more to yourself to be happy, he will be relieved of that burdensome responsibility, and it is much easier for him to give to you when you are already basically feeling good.

A CONSCIOUS MAN:

MEET GAY HENDRICKS, RELATIONSHIP TEACHER

In 1979, I was living with my partner; we had been together for about five years by then. We always ran the same pattern together: one of us would withhold something and then project onto the other. We would get into a big argument and then end up having sex and then do the whole cycle again a couple of weeks later. That was my life with her.

One day I was in the middle of the same argument, and all of a sudden I had the realization: Oh my God! This is not our 500th argument. This is our 500th replay of exactly the same argument. I could finally pull back from the pattern and see it clearly. So I said to her, "Do you want a relationship where we're both honest with each other, where we both take responsibility rather than blame, and where we both focus on our creativity rather than attacking each other? Because attacking is how we spend our energy." God bless her, she said "No!" She said she was only interested in a relationship where I could see that it was all me that was the problem.

There was a cabin on our property, and I went there for a few days to be alone. I asked myself, What do I really want in a relationship? I just sat there for a while and, finally, I realized that what I really wanted was a relationship where both people were real. I asked the universe directly, What do I need to do to have a relationship like that?

I sat there for days, until I could clearly see that every argument had started with one of us lying, or else withholding the truth about a feeling we were having (like sadness or anger). From that lie we would start to criticize the other, and then the other one would criticize back, and it would go through a huge escalation until we had a big blow-out.

I made a promise then, to myself and to the universe. I said, "Here is what I want to live, and if it is not in the cards for me to have that, then I am o.k. to be alone. But I will not settle for less." We split up that day, as it was clear that we did not want the same things.

Three weeks later I met my wife, Katie, and we have been together now for more than thirty-five years. One of the things that attracted us to each other was this idea of creating a relationship that was not based on patterns of blame, but on a commitment to communicate about ourselves from a place of responsibility. We made a commitment to be honest with each other and to taking responsibility instead of blaming each other.

It took us a year to get clear on what the commitments were that would actually be our guideposts. One of them was being honest and communicating our feelings. Another was taking responsibility for things that come up rather than blaming the other person. Another was the commitment to both of our creativity. These three things made all the difference.

From the moment we made those commitments to each other, it took us two or three years before we could show up impeccably because it's hard stuff to learn. It requires a lot of focus to learn how to speak honestly from a place of no blame all the time. The relationship is like metaphysical surfing, with both of us on the board.

Chapter Four

HE LISTENS LIKE THE SKY

Through listening, a man becomes whole. Listening to another person is often thought of as a moral or social virtue, but it is also a powerful way to move deeper than fleeting thoughts and feelings and to become more stable in the dimension of you that is unwavering, unshakable, silent, and still. When listening without trying to change or fix or alter or persuade but simply to discover more about the other person, you access a balance of both masculine and feminine aspects within yourself. The masculine side is aware, present, and unmoving while the feminine is connecting with what the other is saying through empathy and compassion.

If you walk outside, look up into the sky, and scream, "You haven't rained for a week, you bastard! I have a garden to maintain; you just don't care about me," the sky does not react or start to argue with you. "Whoah bro. Chill. I rained ten days ago. And, if you think about it, when I rain, the water gets stored in the roots of the plants and gets used later." The sky does not block you out, putting fingers in its ears and saying, "La la la la... I can't hear you." The sky does not become desperate for your approval and say, "Oh, I'm so sorry. I will rain right now for you." The sky does not react in any way; it remains spacious and present. Listening like the sky means giving the gift of sustained presence and spaciousness.

There are many dimensions to listening. One is just like the sky: to be still and receive. Simply listening to someone sharing challenges and issues may in itself be the solution that is required. Particularly for a woman, when she feels heard, it produces oxytocin–which lowers stress–and then she discovers that she has the power to solve the problem on her own, or it loses its importance. A Conscious Man has the trust that when someone is emotional or stressed, or when new creative thoughts are rising and dreams are sprouting, a process is working in the other person. He knows that he does not have to interrupt that process to fix it. He simply provides a stable and safe container for it to find its resolution.

Another way is active listening by becoming curious and asking powerful questions so as to draw out more from the person speaking. Ivan Misner, the greatest expert in the world on networking, says that a good networker has two ears and one mouth and uses them all proportionally. "It's something I had to work on and I continue to work on. Especially when it is a topic I really know something about. If someone comes to me with an issue, within thirty seconds I feel I know what the problem is, and I have the solution. And I need to tell them. But if you start to tell someone what they should be doing before you have really heard them, they don't feel heard and they can't listen to your answer. You may have heard the same problem one hundred times before. But it's only when the other person feels heard that you can give them suggestions and ideas. So a Conscious Man uses both ears and his mouth in a two-to-one ratio. I'm still working on that."

Deep Listening

A man can listen in a superficial way but also in a deep way. Deep Listening means to hear every dimension of the other person, both what is said as well as what is implied. It means to hear the words and the emotions underneath them and to hear the general disposition and mood of the person: to hear all of it.

Here is a really simple and obvious example. You go to a family gathering at your parents' house. When you arrive, your mother has done most of the preparations already.

"What can I do to help get ready?" you ask.

"Oh, I've done most of it already by myself. It would have been great if you could have asked me an hour ago. Just do what you want now; I really don't care." If you listen only to the words, you might reply, "Well great, Mom. If you really don't care, I'll just go put my feet up and have a beer." But it would be obvious to anybody that the words do not contain everything she is communicating. She is telling you that she feels resentful, abandoned, or frustrated. She has given up hope of you showing up and being present.

Deep Listening means to hear that she has not felt supported, and even deeper listening would mean to also recognize her difficulty in asking for help. It might mean to reach out and connect with her and give her a hug, to quietly in your heart empathize with her feelings, and only then to look around for some practical task that you could take on.

That was an obvious example that very few men would miss. All day long we are faced with more subtle examples where we are called upon to listen more deeply than just to the words on the surface.

When we get distracted in superficial listening, we can become like an attorney, focusing on the exact meaning of words but overlooking where they are coming from. When anyone says, "You never show up on time," or "You always make such a mess," Deep Listening means to not take the words literally but to see them as an opportunity to validate emotion. This is empathy. Rob Allbee learned this in his work in Folsom Prison with prisoners serving life sentences: "You just sit back and listen to the story, listen to where they are coming from. People want to feel like they matter. I've learned that I can just sit here, and listen, and be authentically engaged simply because I want to give the prisoners the feeling that they matter."

Being fully present means to feel what it is like to be inside the other person's reality, including the fact that they are stressed and overtired and maybe need help and do not know how to ask for it. It means to be able to slip inside the other person's shoes and to feel what it's like to be in there. That is how you fall in love with people.

Deep Listening can be condensed down to three powerful statements. You do not need to say these statements out loud; they can be communicated through the way you show up.

I'm right here.

The first statement is one of presence. It is communicated in the way that you are in your body. "Feel me: I'm here with you."

Tell me more.

The second statement is one of curiosity. It communicates a disposition of wanting to know more. "Help me understand this better."

I've got this.

The third statement is one of action. Again, it does not have to be communicated through words or even doing anything immediately. It is a disposition. Think of Michelangelo's statue of David in Florence. He is sizing up Goliath. He has a certain stance. Michelangelo perfectly captures that moment. David is holding his rock, knowing that he has the skill to take down the giant. He has an expression of calm equanimity and confidence. His whole being is saying, "I can do this. I've got it."

WHAT GETS IN THE WAY?

Here are a few of the unconscious habits we have inherited from our ancestors that may get in the way of deep listening. Once again, there is no need to go into a battle with them. Mindfulness is the key.

Dennis the Defense Attorney

Because the instinctive masculine in all of us is more oriented towards logic and analysis, it is easy to get caught up in a process of cross-examination. When your partner says, "You never spend time with the kids," instead of hearing her expression of frustration, abandonment, and concern, it is easy for a man to reply with "Oh, so you think I never spend time with the kids, do you? Well, I bring to your attention, May 18, from 4:12 till 6:32, when I took the kids bowling with my friend Chuck. I would say that qualifies as spending time with the kids, and therefore, your statement using the word 'never' is inaccurate. I rest my case."

The defense attorney insists on taking the matter to trial, which means having a fight. The more arguments that he comes up with, the more the attorney on the other side is going to be scribbling notes to counter everything he says. The trial can get drawn out for days or even weeks. The key is not to interpret the words as an attack but simply as an expression of feeling. We cannot listen deeply if we are rehearsing a counter-argument at the same time.

There are two aspects to listening deeply. One is to recognize that she is telling you how she feels and trying to illustrate it with a story. Even if the story is inaccurate or exaggerated, she still feels the way that she does. The other way is to look for the elements of truth in what she has said. Then you can say, "You are right. I've been working very hard the last couple of weeks and spending less time with the kids than I would like to. I intend to set that straight this weekend."

Fix-It Phil

Higher testosterone levels cause us men to have a faster reaction time, which prompts us to be more solution and action oriented. If we hear or see a problem, we want to fix it. We are both in the same men's group. If one man describes something that has gone wrong in his life, the rest of us look for solutions to help him. Then that man can synthesize the feedback and see what fits and what does not. He gets clear about what he has to do, as well as what he does not have to do. Once he recognizes the right action to take, it releases dopamine in his brain, and he feels at peace.

It is not the same for women. They are more inclined to talk together about their subjective experience of external situations. Other women might ask, "What did he say then? What did you say to him? How did that feel?" It is an empathetic process of validating feelings, which releases oxytocin. She returns to her heart, and she knows what to do from intuition.

When a woman talks about a problem, men mistakenly assume that she is asking for a solution. He assumes she has already explored everything she could do on her own, and she is unable to solve it by herself. Of course, women will often feel that we are being condescending because we misinterpret her and think that she can't manage by herself. Her strong expressions of feeling also cause us to interpret that the problem is much worse than it really is and that the need for a solution is urgent.

Mike the Multi-Tasker

As men, we have the ability to gather facts and indeed accurately repeat them later, while at the same time dividing our attention to something else as well. For example, when someone is telling you about his or her day, it is actually possible to listen enough that you could repeat back the salient facts while at the same time checking your email or sending a text. Listening to gather information does not have the same effect on the other person as listening deeply with all of you.

Peter the Patriarch

Only a couple of generations ago, we lived together in a society where the man, the head of the family, was always right about everything. His authority and decisions could never be questioned. Even a very Conscious Man still carries the shadow of this habit.

John says: I remember a small thing that happened about a year into my marriage that was pivotal for me. We were taking a walk together. I saw a column of smoke coming from down in the valley, and I said to Bonnie, "It's coming from that house."

"No," she said, "It's coming from a field over there." I was absolutely sure I was right. I assumed she was muddled, foggy headed. When we got a little further down, I saw that she was right. I was wrong. I could feel my brain going through an adjustment right there on our walk: "Okay, get the message that when you're really sure you're right, it does not mean that you are always right." Losing a little confidence that my opinions about things are always correct has been enormously helpful in teaching me how to listen.

Equality Edward

Because men and women are becoming equals in going to work, making money, looking after the children, cooking food, and so many other things, it is absolutely natural for us to assume that we should have complete equality with everything. We assume that this should also be the case with talking about feelings and listening: that men and women should have equal time. But in fact, we have both recognized that a woman benefits much more from having the space to talk about feelings, and a man benefits much more from being able to listen.

John says: A few years into our marriage, I had a thriving therapy practice in Mill Valley. I was really good at what I did because I had learned to listen and ask questions, to be curious, and to not immediately offer solutions. One day, I went home after work. I decided I was going to give my wife one hundred percent of my attention, just like I had done all day with my clients.

When I got home, Bonnie was not in the best mood, and she had a long list of complaints for me. So I showed curiosity, I showed interest, I listened deeply, and I asked questions. There was no defensiveness from my side. However, for every complaint she had, I was making my own list of defenses in my head. For every complaint she had, I had a counter complaint. If she said, "You are home late," I was saying in my head, *Well you came home late last Thursday, and I didn't make a big deal about it.* After about fifteen minutes of listening, she must have listed about twenty complaints, and I now had a counter list of thirty saved up. I was feeling quite upset. So I asked her, "Do you now feel completely heard?" She said she did. I went on to ask, "Would now be a good time for me to share my feelings as well?" I expected her to feel obliged to listen to me after I had spent so much time listening to her.

"No, this wouldn't be a good time," she said. That generated yet another complaint on my long list.

So, trying to remain calm, I asked her, "When would be a good time?" I was on my perfect behavior, but I was ready —like an attorney— to get through my list. I wanted to point out that for every complaint she had, I had a better one. That would equalize things in my mind.

"I don't know," she said, "right now, I just want to bask in the sunshine of your love." Now I felt quite confused. *This woman has just had twenty complaints, and now she wants to bask in the sunshine of my love? How could she feel loved by me if she had so many complaints?*

"Now I'm going to make chicken, peas, and mashed potatoes," she went on. She knew this is my favorite meal. While she was cooking, it was like a Disney movie as though there were little bluebirds flying around her head. As she was singing, I was asking myself, *What happened? Now my wife has become Mary Poppins after saying all these things?* I was perplexed. But the longer I waited, the more I noticed my own tension decreasing. I no longer felt so upset.

That night, I got into bed and curled up to go to sleep. I was still feeling defensive. But I saw her go over to her closet and put on some beautiful lingerie. I knew what that meant. *How can she possibly want to have sex with me after she had all those complaints?* I wondered. But I was not going to say, "No." I never say, "No." We ended up having great sex. We fell asleep.

In the morning, she cuddled up next to me and said, "John, now would be a good time for you to share what you are feeling. What is it you wanted to tell me?" To my surprise, I had nothing to say. All my complaints had disappeared.

That day, I learned that countering her complaints with my own list would have only made the situation worse. By hearing her feelings, without arguing or defending myself, her complaints went away. Her heart opened up to me again. I realized that I really did not have a need for her to listen to me in the same way.

Many couples insist on tit for tat: equal time sharing and listening. That might be helpful in a limited way, but remember—as a man—listening deeply will bring you much more long-term satisfaction than sharing your feelings.

THE PRACTICES

Listen without Meaning

Sometimes you can go alone into nature or just sit on the deck of your house. Listen to the sounds around you. Listen to bird sounds, to traffic sounds, and to the sound of the wind in the trees. As you notice each sound, gently remind yourself that it has no meaning. It is just the sound as it is. Each sound is neither good nor bad. When you practice listening consciously, releasing any attachments to meaning or evaluation, you allow a deeper meaning to emerge from your experience. This is not a meaning that is given by your own thinking or beliefs. Rather, it is a meaning that is intrinsic to life and offers you much deeper value. Then, for the rest of your day, you will be much more present in listening to others. Do this practice alone just for 5 or 10 minutes a day to increase your capacity to listen.

Letting Go of Being Right

Whenever you notice yourself entering into a conflict with anyone, as you see yourself getting caught up in facts and needing to be right, you can ask yourself this important question: "In this moment, would I rather be right, or would I rather do the right thing and give the gift of connection?" Generally, when you enter into even a mild conflict or disagreement, you will notice a feeling of contraction in the chest. The more you practice in this way, the more you will remember to let this feeling of tightness be a trigger and to ask this question: "Do I choose to be right, or do I choose to give the gift of presence?" Most of the time, you cannot do both at once. You need to choose.

Here-Nowing

This is a great short practice that quickly develops both the capacity to listen deeply as well as the ability to stay present with what is happening "here." You can do this with your intimate partner or with any friend. It takes ten minutes total. This is not a practice to solve problems: it is something you do every day for a little while, if possible at the same time.

Here are the instructions:

Partner A: For five minutes, give a commentary on your experience of this moment. Speak about what you can hear, what you can see, and what you can feel in your body. If you have a thought, label it as a thought. Be careful to separate what is really your experience from the evaluation of your experience. For example, "I see that you have beautiful eyes," would be changed to: "I see your eyes, and I'm having the thought that they are beautiful."

Here is an example of what this would sound like:

I can feel the breath coming into my chest.
As I look into your eyes, I notice that they are blue-gray.
I can hear the sound of the birds from outside the window.
I am having a memory of when you were listening to music
yesterday, and you nearly cried.
Now I notice that my breath has become more shallow.
I can feel my feet on the ground.

Partner B: Your job is simply to listen like the sky, in the way we have described. Just listen, without interrupting, either externally or by running a commentary in your mind. Practice deep listening.

Continue like this for about five minutes, and then switch over.

It is important to know that this practice has absolutely no appeal to the logical mind because it is not solving immediate problems. In the same way, if you go to the gym every day and lift weights, it is not useful because you are not lifting something that you actually need to. You are going to put the dumbbell back, exactly where it was. But if you keep going to the gym, regularly, after a few weeks, you feel stronger, and you can lift heavier objects at home as well. In the same way, learning to tell the truth about your experience in this moment and learning to listen deeply are not immediately useful, but they both strengthen muscles that are useful for the rest of your life.

The Venus Talk

You and your partner can agree to sit together for 10 minutes a day. She speaks freely about her feelings, and you simply listen. There is no switching roles; you are both benefiting from this practice by polarizing consciously into masculine and feminine energy. When she speaks without any agenda about her feelings from her day, it releases oxytocin, which reduces stress and increases feminine radiance. When you, as a man, practice deep listening without fixing or improving or changing in any way, you become more deeply grounded in your masculinity. This will increase the polarization between you and the attraction in the relationship.

During the Venus Talk you can just listen, or you can also ask questions that encourage her to speak more about her feelings. Show that you are interested: "Tell me more... I want to understand this better... How did that feel to you?" Assume that your partner is from another planet and that you know very little about what it is like to be her.

When you practice listening during the Venus Talk, you can remember to ask questions that remind her of different feelings she may have had in the day. "What was frustrating for you today? What was disappointing for you? What are your concerns and fears? What was embarrassing for you?" Of course, you should not do this in a structured way; it would sound bizarre. Just keep in the back of your mind that these are four feelings that commonly build up. Then you can also be curious to ask, "What do you wish for?" "What did you want in this situation?" "What do you appreciate?" and "What was good about today?"

FOR WOMEN

We have both seen, again and again, that a woman feels more relaxed, more loved and more connected when she can speak freely about her feelings and her man can listen to her. It is not always easy or automatic for men to listen deeply. Men have all kinds of conditioning–some of which goes back thousands of years–in the nervous system, biochemistry, and social conditioning, to want to withdraw and block things out.

Tell Him What You Want

Men take things more literally than women do and are not always so intuitive about anticipating another's needs. When you want help–or anything–from a man, it helps to tell him what you want more than you might need to with another woman.

There is no greater gift that you can give a man than giving him a task that he can carry out for you or that he can accomplish. A man bonds through action, and he feels good about himself and inspired to give more when he is able to check off a task he has accomplished. This is especially true if it is one that has visibly made you happier. But he needs to know what will make a difference to you.

John says: A few years ago, Bonnie and I were at our ranch, a few hours' drive north of San Francisco. There are several buildings on the ranch, and I was standing with two of the workers, giving them some instructions on what needed to be done. Bonnie came out of the house — about 30 yards away — carrying three bags, all of which looked quite heavy. She called over to us with a big smile and said, "Hi there!" We all looked back at her — also with big smiles — and called out, "Hi Bonnie!" Then we went back to our conversation. She stopped: "Aren't you going to help me?" Instantly all three of us ran over to help her. But as men, we didn't readily assume that she needed help until she asked for it. Generally speaking, if a man does not ask for help, it means he does not want help, so he assumes that this is true for you as well.

Talk about How You Feel

For many men, learning to become a deep listener does not happen overnight. Neither of us started out with great listening skills. It took time to develop them. Even today, we both slip up sometimes and fall back into fixing or defending ourselves. Luckily, we both have very patient and understanding wives, who have supported us with some coaching and reminders along the way. If you like, and if your man would appreciate it too, here are some ways you can cheer him on to become an Olympian listener.

See if you can get in the habit of sharing what you feel for a few minutes every day rather than letting it build up until you feel frustrated and explosive. Take a few minutes to talk about your day, the feelings it has evoked in you, and what it is like to experience the world through your eyes. Give him an opportunity to practice deep listening. We call this a Venus talk. Everybody is a winner. Being able to speak freely about your feelings will release oxytocin for you, which will reduce stress and allow you to return to a flow of love. Listening like the sky for him will bring him centeredness and will allow him to return to feeling spacious and connected with himself. It creates a good foundation for both of you when you feel upset. John says: When we are done, Bonnie will often say, "It felt so good to share all that with you. I feel really you are with me." Then she pulls me in for a hug. It makes me look forward to listening even more deeply the next time.

You can also support a man to learn to listen by recognizing that there is a gradient of difficulty. Of course, it is next to impossible for anyone to edit themselves in the middle of a fight or when feeling very emotional, so recognizing these hurdles is simply helpful for when you practice together.

Easy

The low hurdle would be, "I feel sad/irritated/discouraged/frustrated and there is really no reason for it; it is just how I feel." It is easy for almost any man to hear those words easily, and he will probably immediately become empathetic and want to be there for you.

Medium

The middle hurdle would be, "I feel irritated because of what happened at work today." This is a little more difficult because it triggers his "Phil-the-Fixer" identity. As soon as you illustrate your feeling with an external cause, he will tend to focus on how to fix the problem and give less attention to empathizing with your feelings.

Difficult

For most men, it is much more difficult to empathize and hear your feelings when you attribute them to him as the cause: "I'm feeling really frustrated because you never clean the kitchen, you're always late, and I just can't rely on you because you're such a wuss." For a good man who aspires to become a deeper listener, this is the advanced course. Much more than for a woman, men quickly get defensive and want to argue about the cause-and-effect logic of what you are saying.

When you practice talking about your feelings and listening, you could buffer your statements by reminding him, "You don't have to say anything or fix anything. I just want to share my feelings with you so you know what's going on. Then I feel closer to you."

The feminine in all of us wants deep connection, inclusion, and a fair deal for everybody. So it may seem only fair to you that if you are able to share your feelings for a few minutes, he should be able to do the same. But it does not really work exactly the same the other way. Sometimes people have great difficulty accepting this. If he wants to share his feelings as well, and if you want to listen, it will bring you more intimacy. But it is not really necessary. If you share, and he listens, and you do not switch, this is also great. It will increase the polarity between you and allow you to feel more alive with more chemistry and attraction.

A CONSCIOUS MAN:

MEET JACK CANFIELD, AUTHOR OF *THE SUCCESS PRINCIPLES*

In graduate school we had lessons on listening, but I still was not good at it in my relationships. My natural tendency was to fix and help everybody. It was not until I read *Men Are from Mars,* that I understood that women don't want to be fixed, and they don't want a solution, but instead they want to be listened to, that I took that in. I learned to say, "Tell me more," and really mean it. Soon after I read that book, I had a conversation with my sister, and she just went on and on. "Tell me more," I said. "Tell me more." At the end she told me, "That was the best conversation ever."

When I went to an international speaker's association conference, there was a designation called CSP — certified speaking professional. You give talks; you go to the cocktail party. I remember going to my first meeting and thinking, *Oh, these are great people, the best of the best.* I met everybody and shook hands with all the great speakers. Then I met one of the veterans, a bank president. The first thing he said was, "So you are new to CSP?" I said I was. "What is your name?" he asked. I told him. Then he interviewed me for an hour. I never got to ask him a single question. At the end of that hour, I thought he was the coolest guy on the planet. I loved him. He modeled exactly what it is all about—listening, and being interested.

Recently my wife found a question in a book and asked me, "Are you more interested in being interesting, or more interested in being interested?" If you can be more interested rather than being attached to being interesting, relationships work a lot better. Listening is critical. I was a therapist for years, and you have to listen. And when you coach you have to listen, because sometimes people solve their own problems. You are asking them a set of questions that will lead them to think and explore, questions that allow them to come up with their own answers. When they come up with their own answers, they are more invested in their solutions.

The same thing is true in my relationships with my daughters and my sons. I listen. "How is it going?" It's all I have to ask.

I worked for the head of the Stone Foundation with a man named Billie Sharp. He was brilliant—one of the brightest men I've ever met. One day we had a consultant come in, and Billie invited a few of the staff to keep their mouths shut and listen. We were all in our early twenties. Billie asked the consultant question after question, and all he did was listen. After about two hours the consultant left. We all deeply admired Billy and wondered why he hadn't said anything to impress the consultant with his extensive knowledge. I said, "You never said anything, other than asking questions." Billy responded, "I already know what I know. I wanted to know what he knew." That answer left a deep impression on me and still guides me today to be more interested than incteresting.

Chapter Five

HE FEELS HIS WOUNDS BUT IS NOT RUN BY THEM

Whatever affects you from the past that you are not aware of will run your life. If your mother went through an emotional rollercoaster that terrified you, you learned to shut down, freeze, and protect yourself. Later, if your wife or a coworker has expressed out-of-control emotions, you will instinctively freeze and restrict your freedom of expression. A man who freezes, or isolates himself in the presence of strong feelings, becomes weak and afraid.

We do not only carry feelings from the past, but we were also taught how to deal with feelings. Your mother or your father may have told you, "You shouldn't feel that... Big boys don't cry... Well behaved boys don't get aggressive... or revengeful. Happy, healthy boys don't get moody..." Equally, either parent may have tried to buy you out of what you were feeling: "Don't cry; let me buy you an ice cream." Either way, most men did not adequately learn that when they do not get what they want and feel sad, frustrated, angry, or disappointed, those feelings pass quickly. They appear briefly, and then they are gone again.

A man who has lost his capacity to feel, moment to moment, will inevitably have a limited capacity to empathize with what other people are feeling as well. Hurt people, who cannot feel their pain, tend to hurt other people. When a man is not aware of what he is feeling, he tends to diminish it, to ridicule it, to put it down and then seek for action-oriented solutions instead of simply experiencing the feeling and allowing it to pass. The more he is not aware of his own pain, the more difficult it is to hear the pain of another. He wants it all to go away quickly.

As men and women have come to blend the traditional roles from a few decades back, this is now a much greater challenge for men than it is for women. When a woman is under stress, some studies have shown that she has eight times more blood flow to the emotional part of the brain. The limbic system is more extensive in a woman. So she has a much greater capacity to feel and express feelings.

As a man has a limited capacity to feel, he also tends to diminish or ridicule his partner's feelings. This can easily lead to a ping-pong match of distrust. As soon as a woman senses that she is not welcome to express what she is feeling, she loses trust and becomes critical. The man then seeks to defend himself against the criticism and to argue with the logic of what she is saying. She hears this as a further invalidation of her feelings and becomes even more critical while he becomes even more defensive. This is how most conflicts erupt between a man and a woman: they egg each other on in a spiral of distrust.

As soon as you even begin to learn, as a man, how to recognize what you are feeling and how to label it and communicate it skillfully, this breaks the cycle. Your ability to feel cuts through the need to take action or to defend yourself based upon logic. When you feel criticized, you can experience a fleeting sensation of deflation, take a breath, and let it go. There is no need to invalidate what the other is feeling. You can listen and accept it as it is. Disagreements last for a few minutes and quickly turn into laughter instead of a painful standoff that can last for hours or days. As you just begin to learn how to feel, pain becomes a motivator for transformation; it becomes a positive loop. The more you can feel, the more your pain informs you of what you need to adjust in your life, the more you can put your life in balance, and the less pain you need to face. Sounds good? It is. Read on...

All men have feelings, ranging from shame and humiliation, to anger and outrage, to tenderness and compassion. The primary difference between different men is not what we each feel but our capacity to be with it and express it in a way that works for everybody. Every man, consciously or unconsciously, wants to express painful feelings and be free of them. If he does not know how to feel and communicate, he will do it indirectly. This is the principle of "Let me show you how bad it feels, motherf**ker." If he feels humiliated, he will seek to cause that person humiliation as a way of saying, "See, this is what I'm feeling, and it's painful." But revenge generally turns into an escalating cycle instead of resolving painful feelings through experiencing and then communicating.

His and Her Way to Feel

There is a masculine and feminine way to be with feelings. A Conscious Man can access both of these and find the balance that works best for him.

The feminine way to be with feeling is something like surfing. You go with it. When a woman feels angry or sad, she has a greater capacity to allow the feeling to take her over completely. And the more easily she can do this without restriction, the more it will carry her home into feeling herself again: into love as a river discharges into the ocean. So long as no one is trying to talk her out of it and invalidating her feeling in some way, all feelings become a portal into a greater love.

The masculine way to be with feelings is to hold a space bigger than the feeling in which it can arise and pass and then dissipate again. The sense of presence and space is always just a little greater than the feeling.

When you feel contracted, small, wrapped up in your own beliefs and identity, any strong feelings — in you or in another — will cause you to enter into a panic of self protection. The more oceanic you feel, by taking space regularly and feeling connected with yourself, the greater your capacity to experience feelings as they arise, just like a wave in the ocean.

If a man goes too much into following feelings, which might be more suited to a woman, he becomes lost, confused, and uncentered. If he goes too much into watching, he can become cold, analytical, and insensitive. When a man rejects or denies his painful emotions, he shuts himself off from being emotionally alive in general. If you cannot feel anger or grief, you also cannot feel joy or excitement; you can't feel anything.

He needs to find the balance of these two ways that is right for him.

A Conscious Man recognizes that a woman has a much greater need to express feeling than he does. A woman resolves emotional tension through fully feeling it, fully expressing it, and following it all the way home to love. But a man resolves emotional tension by remaining present with it, holding space around it, understanding the message it has for him, and then taking action based upon that feeling to restore balance.

Being present with painful feelings or defensive reactions brings two distinct benefits that support each other. One is this: your increased awareness of your own feelings allows you to also empathize with what another is feeling, and this compassion is a context where resolution happens naturally. Two is this: you become less reactive, and you can use clear thinking to find the best solution.

I Feel Your Pain

As soon as you have a little space around feelings, not only do you have awareness of your own feelings, but you can also empathize with the other. This is neither the old way of repressing feelings and acting tough, nor does it mean acting out feelings by becoming emotional. When a Conscious Man feels criticized, for example, he has learned — through practice — to experience the outer event, to experience his reaction to it, and then to do the right thing anyway.

> *Here I am, coming home, opening the front door. Here is my wife; here are my children. Here she is telling me that I am late. Oh, now she is telling me that I am always late. Here comes the contraction in my chest. Looks like I'm feeling hurt. Here's a thought, moving in with great speed, scrambling to argue with her. It wants to say, "I'm not always late. It's more like 27% of the time." Now I am noticing the frustrated look in her eyes. Here is a softening feeling in my chest. Here I am reaching out to hold her. Here is my wife crying softly. And here comes the kiss.*

This capacity to observe external things and equally to observe emotions, allows the freedom to do what is best for everybody. It is the difference between "I am angry" and the experience of anger as a passing feeling.

When anyone is upset with you, if you can first feel your own reactivity and hold awareness of the story you are telling yourself, it allows you to be sensitive and aware of what is happening in the other person. You cease to be revengeful, or reactive, because you can start to put yourself in the other person's shoes. Because the nervous reactivity is diminished, you can lean in and experience the other's reality and discover what is going on for that person. If you can listen to your own feelings first, then you can listen to another person's feelings as well.

It is no longer necessary to act things out, but it is also no longer necessary to make them go away. You do not have to get rid of "negative feelings" any more then you have to get rid of clouds passing in the sky. You can watch them; they will pass. The reactive feelings that can so easily take life, and get us entangled in endless drama, are revealed to be no more than a mouse with a megaphone.

The Message in Pain

It often happens that once we are able to create some space around feeling in this way, we automatically become aware of the story hidden just underneath. John says: Sometimes my wife complains about me. She thinks I have not done enough around the house. Then I feel like withdrawing. As I withdraw from her, I ask myself, "Why am I pulling away?" It is because I am feeling pain. "What kind of pain am I feeling?" Quickly, I discover that there is a story lurking there, that she does not appreciate what I say or do just because she made that one comment. I have an opportunity to question, to inquire. Does it really mean that she does not appreciate me? Or could it just mean she's not feeling so good today? It gives me the opportunity to not take it personally. When I was less aware of my feelings, I used to withdraw for a few days at a time. Now, I can question it immediately, upgrade my interpretation, heal it almost instantaneously, and connect again. If I can feel my pain, I can question my interpretation of what she just said, and I can ask if the interpretation is true. Being able to feel pain not only means you do not have to react, but it also means that you can upgrade your interpretation of events so you do not feel the same pain in the future. We can cease to tell ourselves painful stories.

The more that a man restores his ability to fully experience feeling, the more he can connect with a deeper level of feeling, one that is connected to what is happening here in this moment rather than something left over from the past. We all have a way that our soul communicates to us. It is not with words. Your soul is your conscience; it tells you what is good and where to go. It says "Yes" to this and "No" to that. When you have gone off track, or when something in your environment is off track, you know about it because you have a warning-signal emotion. Painful emotion can simply be a way to tell you what needs fixing. Your capacity to fully experience feeling without becoming reactive reconnects you to intuition, to your inner compass that guides you to the true North.

WHAT GETS IN THE WAY?

Here are some of the parts of us that may have gotten locked in the basement and get in the way of feeling pain and letting it go.

Avoidance Arthur

At the most primitive level, our whole motivation as men is to avoid feeling pain at all costs. In the past, men have found ways to avoid difficult feelings through opiates, alcohol, marijuana, sexual addiction, intellectualization, and over thinking. Just about any compulsive activity can become addictive, and it is all fueled by an instinct to avoid pain. A good first step is to take a journal and start to catalog the ways that you avoid painful emotions. The more you can get these onto paper and recognized, the less power they will have over you. Here are a few ideas from our side to get you started, but just use this just as a springboard into your own exploration of the huge momentum we all share of dulling ourselves emotionally:

1. *Arguing, over thinking, and the need to be right*
2. *Alcohol and other substances*
3. *Distraction: watching TV or cruising the Internet*
4. *Addiction to work*
5. *Extreme sports or dangerous situations*

Now you fill out your own list.

Invalidation Victor

As men, we can instinctively think that there is no reason to get in touch with feelings: it does not do anything useful and it has no purpose or value. A man's first reaction in his primitive brain, when there is danger, is to either fight or run. This is how he responds in anticipation of pain, and it was the most intelligent response when men lived as hunters faced continuously with physical danger. Stopping to feel could be a suicidal step. Because of her very different role in the social fabric in the past, a woman's first reaction when faced with pain is "I need to tell somebody about it." Her first reaction is expression.

Still today, men often see feeling as a sign of weakness: "Real men don't cry." The key to becoming a Conscious Man is to be aware of your emotional, feminine side but without letting it run your life. By becoming aware of your emotions as well as the cooler analysis of the best action to take, you allow the feminine side of you to support the masculine. Only by becoming aware of feelings can you have the presence to understand that you do not have to act on them. They will dissipate and reveal another part of your humanity: you can become more sensitive, more considerate, and more compassionate.

Blurt-It-Out Bart

Just as we can sabotage ourselves as men by invalidating our feelings, we can also lose our way by getting lost in feeling if we have not built a large enough container in which the emotions can move. In order for a man to fully feel his feelings and not act on them, he has to have a way to experience the feelings without being threatened or overwhelmed by them. We will share with you some practices to increase your ability to experience feelings within a greater sense of space.

Without ways to develop presence, you may feel compelled to blurt out from feeling emotional before even experiencing what you are feeling. It is a little like premature ejaculation. You need to develop the stamina to contain your energy so that it can be released at the right time and in the right way.

Disembodied Dave

The way to experience feelings, without becoming emotionally reactive and getting caught up in drama, is to experience them through the body.

Men today often sit for hours looking at computer screens and following a sedentary lifestyle. Ultimately, you get free of pain and the past by stabilizing yourself, more and more deeply, into the tangible reassuring reality of the present moment. This is where the body lives. If you spend a lot of time sitting and thinking, you may need to find ways to move, to breathe, and to become more alive.

THE PRACTICES

As we grow more in conscious masculinity, we discover that we can transform pain into pleasure simply by staying present. The charge of negative emotion dissipates just by holding it and by not resisting it. A man who has learned to endure painful experiences, both physical and emotional, becomes an enduring man, a man others can count on.

Emotional Endurance Training

This is not only something modern; it is part of a process of initiation in many old cultures. At puberty, a boy enters into manhood through a rite of passage: sometimes an excruciatingly painful event by learning to feel pain without taking action to remove it. In the Mandan Tribe that lived along the Missouri River, for example, the Okipa ceremony involved piercing the breast of a boy with a wooden hook before the whole community. He could not cry out; he would have to learn how to endure pain and to hold it. The word "endure" comes from the Latin root "in" plus "durus," which means to make hard. Enduring any difficult feeling causes a man to become stronger. They would then throw a rope over the limb of a tree, tie the rope to the stick, and pull the boy upward from his chest, so he would lift off the ground. He was hanging in the air all day but not able to cry out. If he could go through this process, he became a man. He learned to feel pain, not to seek out comfort, not to run away, and not to express feelings. He had to learn how to hold it, how to feel inside himself, and how to endure. In this way, a boy became a man: by learning that when he stays present with something as long as it exists, it will dissipate. If you feel pain in your body, without reaction, it will produce endorphins and give you bliss.

Today, many men are constantly running away from pain. We were not encouraged to feel pain as boys if nobody was listening to us, so we stopped listening to our own pain. However, if a boy has a parent who can embrace and hold him when he is in pain, he will gain the ability to hold his own pain. Rob Allbee tells us that the prisoners he works with in San Quentin never had that. They did not learn how to embrace pain. So either they have to run away from their pain or inflict it on someone else. Once you learn to feel, you know that when your pain levels go up and you can stay present with them, endorphins get produced.

In coaching men, we have not guided anyone through the Okipa ceremony of the Mandan Tribe. We do not specialize in suspending teenage boys from hooks in the chest. But we have found all kinds of ways to help a man increase his capacity to endure painful feelings, long enough that they transform into pleasure and into presence. We have learned a lot about how a man can develop emotional endurance.

One excellent method is to hold your body in the same position for several minutes without moving. Many people today are discovering the powerful benefits of the ancient Chinese discipline of Chi Kung. Putting your body into the "tree posture" for five or ten minutes will feel uncomfortable at the beginning, but even after a few weeks of practice of learning to endure uncomfortable feelings, you develop greater inner strength as well as the ability to hold presence for another person. Yoga works in the same way.

Listen without Reaction

We have already suggested several practices to develop deep listening skills. Now you can integrate them with the capacity to endure painful emotions without reacting. When someone is upset with you, experiment with staying present and listening without exercising the need to defend yourself. Rest the hand on your lower belly, and breathe deeply enough so that it pushes your hand out. As you notice difficult feelings arising within you, let go of any thoughts or arguments, and simply feel them as physical sensations. Important: do not try and do this practice for more than five or a maximum of ten minutes at a time. It can be more challenging than you might imagine.

The Feeling Letter

Once feelings have come to the surface in this way, take some time to be alone. Anchor yourself in your body, relax your breathing, and feel the sensations associated with what you are feeling. As you feel the sensation, ask yourself what emotion is associated with the physical sensation, and write it down. Label it.

Now ask yourself the question: "If that part could speak, what would it say?" Give yourself free reign here to be unedited. No one is ever going to read this. If you like, you can write it on a loose piece of paper and then tear it up or burn it later. What does this part of you want to do, knowing that you are not going to do it in real life? Give yourself permission to be revengeful, dark, and ugly. It is only a letter. Make sure you include these questions:

*What am I angry about? What would I like to do about it if
there were no consequences?
What am I sad about?
What am I afraid of?
What do I regret?*

These are four emotions that are commonly inhibited. After some
minutes, when you feel you have freely journaled these four emotional
states, including all the fantasies of how you would like them to act out,
you can shift to asking yourself this:

What is it that I truly want or wish?

Then you can move to this:

*What do I appreciate? Where do I have forgiveness? Where do
I feel love? What do I want to apologize for?*

Distilling the Truth

Another way to be present with strong feelings is to use your power of
discrimination to differentiate leftover feelings in the past from the actuality
of the present moment. This is a very simple exercise that does not require
much practice or understanding. It only requires deep emotional courage. If
you find it too challenging to go through these steps on your own, it would
be very easy to get together with a buddy and make an agreement to guide
each other when you need to.

Here are the steps:

1. Go to a place where you can be alone, and either stand in a posture
   without moving, or sit down.

2. Scan your whole body and look for places of emotional contraction or upset.

3. Label the emotion you are feeling such as anger, sadness, frustration, or hopelessness. Stay with this feeling for a couple of minutes until you can recognize that it exists on its own.

4. What stories are involved with this emotion? Now go deeper by asking yourself why you feel that way. For example, if you feel angry, you might discover that your anger has woven the web of a story like "My wife is unfair to me." Or a feeling of sadness might create a story like "Nobody understands me; I am all alone."

Once you have identified the story you simply have to ask yourself, "Is this true?" You can also ask, "Can I let this story go?"

In order for something to be objectively and factually true, it would be necessary for everybody on the planet to agree. Unless all of your friends agree that your wife is unfair to you, and she agrees too, or that nobody understands you, it is only an opinion.

The stories and beliefs will unravel on their own, and then the painful feelings will naturally dissipate.

John says: Before I was married to Bonnie, I lived with another woman for a few years. When we argued, I would get upset and storm out of the house. I was not aware of my feelings inside. I was just overtaken by the sense of "I'm done with this." I would slam the door as I left the house, get in my car, and drive to a hotel. By the time I got to the hotel, I had calmed down a little bit, and I was more in control of myself. I became rational: "Why am I going to spend money on a hotel, when I can sleep at home? We have a spare room." So I would turn the car around, creep back inside, and go to another room to sleep. The next day I would wake up, and everything was fine.

The next time it happened, I also slammed the door as I left the house and got into the car. Now I asked myself, "Why am I going to a hotel? I know I'm not going to stay there." So I just sat in the car. Then I would calm down, and eventually sneak back into the house and go to the other room to sleep.

The story goes on like this many times, until I would walk down the stairs, open the door, and slam it without stepping outside at all. I was thinking "I know I'm not going anywhere, so why do I even have to step outside?" I was only slamming the door so she would feel sorry and want me to come back.

Then I learned another step. I did not even need to even get upset. I could just say to her, "Listen, I feel like I'm getting upset by this argument. I'm going to go and sleep in the other room, and I'll talk to you tomorrow. Please don't come after me. I need some space." The result was just the same. The next day everything was okay. Through discrimination, I learned to anticipate my needs, and these reactive feelings diminished.

Developing Compassion

Often, you can let go of difficult feelings, which are woven together with memories from the past, by going through a simple process of compassion and forgiveness. The steps are very simple, and you can do them on your own or ask a friend to guide you through them. You can also read the steps here: arjunaardagh.com/no-other.

FOR WOMEN

When men are in pain, the first tendency is often to withdraw and pull away. It is the primitive reaction of fight or flight. If a man feels trapped, instinctively he moves into defense or even into attack. So if you have a fight with your man, or if you simply get upset and he wants to withdraw, let him do so and do not go after him. If you chase after him, he is going to have to continue running. The best thing you can do to encourage conscious masculinity in your partner is to ignore him when he takes space to feel and do something else to make yourself happy. For many women, this may mean talking about what you are feeling with another woman. But of course, you have found your own ways to feel good within yourself.

We have discovered that because women are instinctively more relational than men, they often want to pursue a man when he withdraws. You may want to ask, "What's the matter?... What's going on?... What did I do wrong?... Let's talk about this..." All of these may be good questions once he has come out of the cave again. Anything that you do or say with the intention of bringing him out of the cave before he is ready will easily cause him to pull further away. If your partner knows how to take space when he is upset but also knows how to come back when he is balanced and ready to connect with you again, please be grateful that you have found yourself a Conscious Man.

Don't Punish Him

After a man withdraws to allow feelings to dissipate through stillness and he comes back to his partner, she sometimes gets mad at him and tells him that he has hurt her. Her hope is to change him from ever pulling away from her in that way again. Of course, a good man does not want to hurt you, and at the same time we are all learning how to be the best men we can be in a rapidly changing environment. So if brief periods of withdrawal for centering are met with anger or even feelings of hurt, it will discourage him from taking space again, which in the long run may simply lead to more fighting for longer periods of time.

Don't Push Him to Talk about Feelings

A man can get easily confused when you want him to share what he is feeling. Remember, our biology is different. Talking about feelings releases stress for you, but it may not be the same way for him. If you tell him he is emotionally withdrawn, he may believe you. If you do manage to get him to engage with you to frequently share feelings, particularly feelings of vulnerability or sadness or despair, and if you do successfully engage him in talking about difficult things from his past, you may feel closer to him. But you may also come to view him as a weak man and lose respect for him. John and I have both seen this happen so often. If you feel that your partner is carrying a lot of painful feelings within himself, you can request him or encourage him to take action to deal with that. This might even involve going to see a psychotherapist. If he can logically see that this will improve the quality of his life, he may be willing to take that action on his own. Be careful about becoming the soft shoulder for him to cry on; you may end up with another girlfriend instead of an attractive man.

Acknowledge When He Does Not Act on Upset Feelings

As we are all changing so much in the way that we relate with each other, we are in a kind of a school together. Most of the men we know are in an active and noble process of learning how to be conscious and giving men. If you have a fight, and he has the opportunity to be angry and hurtful with you or to slam the door and leave or to act out his pain in all kinds of ways, and he does not do any of that, find a way to acknowledge him.

For both of us, it is been a long process to learn how to back away when it is time to calm down, how to be present with feelings so they dissipate, and then how to come back to our partners with something new to give. If your man learns how to do this, or is even taking the first steps in learning how to do this so that arguments and fights get less frequent and shorter in duration, please tell him that you appreciate it. Honor him for his successes, and he will rapidly grow in his ability to show up as a conscious and present man for you: "I appreciate that you backed off and took some space when you were upset."

If you are single, a man who acknowledges feelings but does not dwell on them will be a man you can trust. As you get to know him better, if he tells you about challenging situations where he felt humiliated, attacked, or criticized, and he tells you that his response was to back off, breathe, and feel, then you can trust that he will do the same later with you if you get closer to him. A man who angers quickly, who gets confrontational when challenged, and who feels insulted or gets moody, will almost without doubt also do that with a partner he is close to.

A man who talks a lot about his feelings, cries with you, or wants to process his feelings with you, may feel really good to you: intimate, close, and safe. But we want to tell you that in our experience, such a man quickly becomes less attractive to a woman once she gets to know him. Equally, a man who has no emotional reaction at all to powerful events in his life, especially a man who claims to have transcended his feelings through some kind of spiritual practice, is likely to be cold and not empathetic with you as you get closer to him. A Conscious Man worthy of your heart's opening can feel his own feelings, feel with another as well, and still Do the Right Thing anyway.

A CONSCIOUS MAN:

BILL KAUTH, FOUNDER OF THE MANKIND PROJECT

I was born at the time when it was quite acceptable for parents, even good parents, to have relatively little contact with their children. My father was raised on a farm, so he was the kind of guy who was always working. I rarely spent any time with him, except for a couple of fishing trips. The medical world at that time separated children from their mothers at birth. Babies were put away in a bassinet in another room, breaking the mother-child bond. Furthermore, my mother was influenced by Dr. Spock theory that you should only feed a baby every three hours, no matter how much they screamed. So although I never knew it consciously, I developed a lot of pain around wanting bonding and not getting it.

This pain led me to endlessly seek solace with women. But I did not know how to receive love, so I kept moving from one woman to another. This pattern got me into a lot of trouble, and I hurt a lot of women because I was seducing and abandoning. I could never let myself feel and receive the love that I was looking for. It was an addiction not unlike alcoholism, when your life becomes unmanageable. When I finally recognized the pain I was causing women and myself, I just stopped it. Done. I made a vow to not be with women for a long time, and it lasted for well over a year. I found some peace through this celibacy.

A friend said to me, "Lets build a men's group." "What is a men's group?" I asked. He knew I had some training from graduate school in working with groups. So we did it. We got a group of men together, taught some basic communication skills, and made a commitment to stay together for a while. Once we had built enough safety that we could risk speaking out, one of the men said to me, "Bill, you may be a great group leader and facilitator, but you are out of touch with your body. You need to do some bodywork." I was not happy to hear this, but I took it in because I knew he loved me enough to tell me the truth.

I found a bioenergetic therapist and began working with him. In the second session he asked me to get into the "stress position." He showed me how to do it: bowing your back with your hands on your hips and tipped way backward. It is a very uncomfortable position to stand in. Eventually your leg starts shaking from the strain of holding your body up, and then you drop out of your head into your body. I exploded into tears.

In the group that week we had been talking about my dad. I came back the following week, and twenty minutes into the session we talked about my dad again and I started crying. I felt all this anguish I had no clue was there.Ê That was the beginning of my opening heart. That was the first experience where I could really feel my wounding.

I cannot lie to you and say that this was all healed in one magical moment. It went on for years and years. I was leading the New Warrior Training eight times a year, and anytime anybody had something come up about fathers and sons, I would start crying again. I must have spent hundreds of hours crying over stories about people not connecting.

At some point I had felt it deeply enough that it lifted. Ten years ago I met Zoe, who is now my wife. I remember praying to myself that it will work out, and sure enough it did. We were both mature enough that finally, for the first time in my life, I could allow myself to really be loved. I broke the chain.

Chapter Six

HE TRANSFORMS HIS ANGER INTO POWERFUL LEADERSHIP

We do the things we most regret when we are angry. Anger is activated by the back part of the brain, the reptilian brain — the seat of the fight or flight response — and often inhibits our ability to make rational decisions from the prefrontal cortex. So without some conscious training, when a man gets angry, he is most likely to do and say things that will not only cause him pain, but cause pain to others as well. This then later causes him to realize that he made a bad decision.

What happens when we get angry? Because anger often bypasses rational thought, we may react instinctively in ways that helped us survive in the far distant past but are now counterproductive. In dangerous times, anger could intimidate, control, establish the dominant alpha male position, or stop an enemy, by displaying a willingness or intent to become violent. In this manner, anger was then and often still is a primitive form of communication.

Getting angry was a way to warn someone that if they continued their behavior, they would suffer in some way. If the unwanted behavior continued, then the violence that followed was also a form of communication. Its message was, "Now that I have hurt you, you know how I feel. So don't do it again." (Ironically, for the primitive man, violence was his attempt at sharing his feelings.)

Primitive feelings of anger are not only a way for a man to stop somebody from hurting him but also a way of asserting control through intimidation. We have all seen mafia movies: the mob boss walks in and looks around in a menacing way. If someone just coughs the wrong way, the boss shoots him in the head. It is a way of saying to the whole community, "You don't mess with me. Don't cause me any harm, or even feelings of irritation, because this is what will happen to you. It is a warning: don't cause me to feel bad."

A man can also get angry when his perceived needs are not getting met, when his safety is not assured, and he does not know what to do. It is a message from the soul saying, "Something is happening right now that I don't like and I don't want." But he often skips over what that is. He might want somebody to love him and appreciate him, but instead he feels insulted or threatened. He strikes out in anger before even realizing that he missed feeling loved. He goes directly into anger without experiencing the moment before, when he felt hurt or threatened or that his needs were not getting met.

Our history is for a man to try and establish the dominant alpha-male position: to create a pecking order through violence. If he got angry, raised his voice, intimidated and frightened people, or demonstrated that he could hurt, he established himself as the man with the most power and the one least subject to harm. Such a man thinks that he has the greatest freedom to express himself and to look after those close to him.

Another element in our history of violence is the pleasure of revenge. We have all seen Hollywood movies. The bad guy kills a helpless mother and child. The father is on fire and hunts the killer down. It goes through an endless series of turns before they end up on a bridge somewhere, fighting to the death. Finally, the father commits an enormous act of violence, way beyond what he is revenging. He throws his opponent off the bridge, where the villain lands on a spike that sticks straight up through his body. The whole scene is extraordinarily gory. Our reaction to the first murder was anger and disbelief. Our reaction to the revenge is satisfaction. It is the principle of an eye for an eye. If an innocent has been wronged, or hurt, and if someone can exact a similar or greater hurt, it creates justice, and the second violence gives us pleasure.

We have celebrated the image of the violent man; women find him sexy. Both men and women go to movies where you see Jason Bourne or James Bond randomly killing anonymous people, and we feel admiration. It gives us the image of the strong man, not a wimp. He does not back down, cannot be dominated, and is a protector. He protects his woman and the people close to him, and he protects what is right. He protects through violence. As men, we have been trained to think this man of violence is a cool guy.

What happens in the movies does not translate very well to regular life. In the movies, the great hero can randomly shoot people. If you try to do that in regular life, you will end up going to prison. Acts of violence are not condoned in real life.

His and Her Anger

Because of higher levels of estrogen, when a woman is angry or feels threatened, she feels a greater need to talk, share her feelings, and get help. Talking about her feelings increases oxytocin, which helps to lower her stress. If she does not feel heard or validated, blood flow dramatically increases to the hippocampus, the part of the brain associated with memory. Under increasing stress, she will experience selective memory, forget any good thing he has ever done, and remember in full Technicolor with Dolby surround sound every mistake he has ever made. Her words are critical and sound to him like a character assassination. She may say mean things or go as far as to throw things, but she is less likely to physically attack with force.

For a man it is different; blood flows to the action centers in the brain. Because he is running on testosterone, if he loses control of the primitive part of the brain, his anger propels him into action. When he gets out of control, he may even commit physical violence.

She hurts through words; he hurts through action.

For example, Marcy and Tom get into an argument about how much time Tom spends away at work and on the computer at home. Feeling rejected, Marcy says, "I should never have married you. You're always late, you never pay attention to me, you don't take any care of the kids, and you're a lousy father — and a terrible lover."

Tom takes these things very personally and literally. He feels outraged because he thinks they are not true. He feels a need both to stop her attack yet also show her just how wrong she is and how much her words hurt him. At that point, if he does not give himself permission to temporarily walk away and cool off, his anger increases, and because he feels he has no escape, he lashes out. Hurt people hurt other people.

Dominate or Be Dominated

Both in personal relationships and at work, a man frequently finds himself in a situation where the choice seems to be to dominate or to be dominated.

Either get angry and inflict pain — or use the threat of pain — to gain control of the situation, or lie down, roll over, and let people walk all over you. In the past, this was a no-brainer: use force and anger to win the war, each and every time. Be a real man.

For men today, however, who are seeking to become more conscious, this creates a new dilemma.

He feels guilt for the anger that wells up in him, and then, because in the reptilian part of the brain the choice seems either to dominate or be dominated, he backs down and becomes submissive. It seems to be the only way to deal with the anger within him for which he feels ashamed.

When a man loses power in this way, the enzyme aromatase is released, which converts his testosterone into estrogen. At a biochemical level, he actually becomes more feminine. A man who has become passive or soft in this way is much less likely to get angry, but when he does, he is more likely to explode. The higher estrogen makes him more emotional and more likely to lose control.

Arjuna says: A few years ago I was featured in *Awake in the Dream* a film made by the talented Austrian filmmaker Nina Roland. It won the Grand Jury Prize at a film festival in Frankfurt. As a result, my seminars became more popular in German-speaking countries, and I offered coaching to many men there. Although the war was over in 1945, more than seventy years ago, there is still collective shame carried in Germany and Austria. They went through a period, still in living memory, of giving full expression to hyper-masculine force, anger, and extreme violence. The entire culture was defeated and shamed by the whole world. For many years after the war, Germany needed babysitting from other nations as the Germans were deemed unfit to govern themselves. Therefore, even today German-speaking men have amputated not only their violence and acting out with anger, but they have also — to a great degree — cut off their power, authority, and ability to take bold action. Women in Germany complain that most of the men there are soft, over-empathetic, and indecisive. When I work with such men, the challenge is not to dissipate their anger but to wake up this primal force again, play with it, and learn to integrate it as the much-needed foundation for powerful and decisive leadership. It is also needed for creating a healthy and polarized relationship with a woman.

The dilemma that modern men all over the world face today, both with other men, in the pecking order at work, and at home, is this: is he going to dominate or be dominated? Both feel undesirable. When he dominates, he becomes the old style macho guy who never feels or shows emotion, is hard, and is capable of committing violence without feeling another's pain with no empathy. Or he learns to feel, which makes him more empathetic, but this can also frequently lead to him being dominated and wishy-washy: he becomes the beta man at the bottom of the pecking order.

The Magic Key

The solution is the magic of consciousness. Being mindful is the key. A Conscious Man transcends the dilemma, to dominate or be dominated, by developing the capacity to feel and bring anger alive within him without having to mindlessly react. You move beyond the impossible choice. You can fully feel your anger, and you are able to explore more deeply. If you get rejected and feel angry, rather than mindlessly rejecting back, you can access your original intent of the best for everyone and have the choice to find another way to boldly and fearlessly achieve your positive intention. You transcend the duality of unconscious expression or unconscious suppression, which were both equally automatic.

To act out without awareness, or to suppress without awareness, are equally expressions of unconscious masculinity. The fight or flight response comes unconsciously from the reptilian brain. Meanwhile, emotional responses, including empathy as well as reactivity, come from the limbic part of the brain. Cool, rational, logical awareness is associated with the prefrontal cortex. Each of these on its own would be imbalanced.

To be conscious means that the whole brain is activated. The reptilian brain is active because you are still able to feel righteous anger, righteous indignation. This provides power, energy, and motivation. At the same time, your limbic system is active because you can feel your own emotions yet also empathize with others. This can give you a greater motivation to care about others and the ability to feel what you really want. The prefrontal cortex allows you to make conscious choices about how to best take action and when to hold back: to create an outcome best for yourself and everyone else as well. This naturally creates trust in everyone around you in your capacity to take leadership. They know you have their backs.

Feeling anger without immediately acting on it may sometimes involve you taking a breath to relax the tendency to yell but also communicating firmness. Or you may simply back off and take a breath. By feeling and being aware of your anger without acting on it, you are learning to honor your mission and purpose and to stay on track. In this way, you convert your anger into authoritative leadership. You now have the capacity to not just be taken over by emotion but to also recognize what you are feeling, which is a different thing. Awareness of anger is very different from being angry. Feeling anger, rather than simply being angry, leads to becoming more aware of what someone else is feeling as well. When we become emotionally charged, when we "are angry," we cannot feel other people because we have been too taken over by our own emotion. We become oblivious to what is going on around us. But when you experience emotion together with awareness, you can say to yourself, "Right now I am feeling angry." Only then can you also recognize, "This other person is feeling threatened; that is why he/she is speaking and acting this way, which is provoking anger in me." This insight, that comes from empathy, can soften the tendency to strike back and instead inspire great leadership: the intelligence and creativity to find a better outcome for everyone.

Anger becomes compassion. You become a more trustworthy leader, more so than either the angry, action-oriented macho man of the past or the overly empathetic, soft man, who denies feeling anything but love, peace, and apology.

Healthy Remorse

When you apply this concept to reflecting upon your past, it gives you the benefit of the positive aspect of remorse. Think back to when you hurt somebody in the past, to a moment when you were angry and acted on it. At that time, you might have found ways to justify your actions. With blood flow restricted to the front part of the brain, you could only feel your own pain but not the pain of the other person. Remembering this now, with more blood flow to all of your brain, you will also be able to empathize with the pain of the other person and learn from your experience in the past. What was it that caused that person to behave as they did that made you angry?

What did they feel when you caused them pain? That is how you mature in awareness. You can feel remorse by feeling the pain you have caused.

Now you can learn and grow in your capacity to lead. The next time you are in a situation where you feel anger welling up, you can anticipate that remorse: "When I act out this anger, it will later — perhaps much later — lead to me feeling bad about myself. I will lose people's respect, and it may be hard to win it back again. I will later feel the pain I caused and regret it." The healthy anticipation of remorse becomes a motivator to channel anger into another direction.

Authoritative Leadership

The other benefit for you in learning to feel anger is that you can channel it into firm authority, into raising your voice sometimes in a way that becomes a gift to other people. Arjuna says: I learned this most powerfully when my boys became teenagers. If I became angry, they could see it immediately, and I lost their respect and cooperation. But when I learned to raise my voice and set limits without being taken over by emotion, both of my sons would listen and respond. Now that they are grown and I have graduated from Dad School, I can take this valuable lesson with me into other situations. I have learned the capacity to take leadership with confidence.

The way that you are with other men's anger is a significant factor in how you are with you own anger. If you let yourself be intimidated, if you bow down to another man's anger, feeling it as a threat and letting him win the alpha-male war, the result is that you become dominated and you also lose connection with your own power. By pushing away another man's anger, you also push your own anger into the basement. When you get comfortable with other men's anger, and you are not pushed around by it, you learn to stand firm even if it means standing firm while trembling or even in tears. Just that courage to stand strong in the face of a bully will not only stop you from being the beta male, but it will earn you respect as a leader who has courage as well as an open heart.

Becoming aware of anger allows you to find the positive message in it for everyone. *There is something that I don't like here... There is something that does not work for all of us... someone's need is not being met... a passion is being suppressed... I'm being threatened in some way or someone else is.* It also allows you to realize that anger is energy. If you act on anger when it is coursing through your body, you may become violent, hurt people, and do things you later regret. However, if you let that energy move through your body, it can make you feel more alive. That aliveness becomes authority and trustworthy leadership.

By fully feeling this message and not immediately acting on it, you can then go a little deeper and consciously feel your positive desire for everyone. This positive desire is a source of great leadership and the capacity to motivate. By shifting your perspective from what you do not want to what you do want, you can access a stream of positive energy and creative intelligence. With this new "insight," you can now consciously upgrade the automatic unconscious reactions of the primitive brain to more intelligent and conscious responses.

IN THE WAY

There are a few things a man has to face in order to transform his relationship to anger.

Intimidation Ian

Trying to dominate other people to get our own way is very tempting: it offers short-term gratification. If we want to immediately get things done and if we want to have the immediate satisfaction of not feeling threatened or not feeling vulnerable, it is very tempting to want to claim the top-dog position. Intimidation often works short-term; it is the primitive unconscious self that raises his spear and says threatening things: "You'd better watch out, or you'll get hurt." People will submit because they do not want to get hurt by an angry man. This is a shortcut to dominate and get control. But of course, it also creates distrust, it destroys sustainable relationships, and it stifles the trust needed to lead effectively. We do not get friendly neighbors that way. We get people who are afraid of us, and as soon as there is a chink in the armor, they will gang up together to get their own back.

Depleted Desmond

When a man lets his reserves deplete, he is running on stress hormones, and the blood flow will go first to the reptilian brain and the emotional brain before the frontal cortex. The frontal cortex, which makes decisions, was the last part of the brain to develop, and it is also the last part to get blood flow. When we are stressed, the blood flow will pull back from the frontal cortex, and we become more emotional and move into fight or flight. When we are running on stress, we are more likely to get angry, and it is more likely for that to erupt into violence.

The key is to take a walk when you feel emotional. Recognize that a part of you needs to take a break. Make a mental note to yourself: *I need more rest, I need to pace myself better, and I need more days off.* Sometimes simply noticing this will cause you to immediately relax. Just the thought of *I'm going to take next Sunday off* will allow your nervous system to relax more: right now, today. Great leaders take vacations.

Wimpy Wilfred

Just as we can be taken over by anger in its more destructive aspects, so a man can also become so afraid of and unfriendly with his own anger so that he shuts off the source of his power. Once he has lost his sense of direction and certainty, he feels weak, becomes easily tired and overwhelmed, and instead of offering leadership, his focus moves to pleasing people, seeking approval, and apologizing for his very existence. Rather than transforming his anger into powerful leadership, he denies the source of his anger in shame and becomes a follower of others. The key here is to play with anger, to find ways to celebrate its raw power and aliveness, and to trust that with awareness, no one will come to any harm.

Pathologizing Pete

When you get defensive or angry, it is common for someone to accuse you, "Don't be so defensive," as though that is a really bad thing. Then there is the temptation to think, *I shouldn't be defensive, and I shouldn't be feeling anger.* There is nothing wrong with anger; in fact, it is a good thing. It is the key to accessing your power and ability to lead. It is only what you do with it that is an issue. If you are unaware of it, if you do not realize that you are angry, it will overflow into things that you later regret doing. Trying not to be angry, or defensive, or trying to be pleasant, will just turn you into a wimpy guy who earns no respect. Whenever anyone says, "You are being defensive," it is itself antagonistic. The best response is to say, "It's true. I am feeling angry and defensive. Give me a moment here." When someone says you are being defensive, don't defend yourself. Just recognize that it is true, own it, and say to yourself, "This is good. It is my primary energy. Now I'm going to withdraw and be with it, and treasure it, and I'll come back when I have something good to offer."

Responsible Robert

When life is not fair, when things do not work out, or when everything goes wrong and you feel angry, many men tend to blame someone for it or even blame themselves. Then they feel that they are inadequate. At such a time, put your hands over your chest and take a deep breath. After the exhale, say to yourself, "I am feeling angry. Everyone feels angry." Then remember the deepest wisdom that every great leader, from Buddha to Alexander the Great to Bill Clinton, has handed down throughout the ages: SH*T HAPPENS! Then remind yourself, "We are all good people, doing the best we can."

THE PRACTICES

Timeout

When you notice that you are provoked by any outside stimulus and you have been taken over by anger, the key is to simply say something simple like, "I am feeling a little thrown off center; give me a minute." Another way to say this would be, "I really need some time to think about what you are saying, so let's take some time out." Taking a little time allows you to fully digest the gift of the anger without it turning immediately into action. This is the most essential key to great leadership.

When the blood is no longer flowing to the front part of your brain, you cannot hear what that person is saying to you anyway. They are angry, you are getting angry, you are slipping into reactive mode, and you need to find a way to pull yourself out of it. Do not phrase it like this: "I've had enough of this BS. I'm out of here." That does not work quite as well.

The Empowerment Process

Anger prevents you from thinking clearly, being able to learn lessons, correcting yourself, and hearing another's point of view. Fight or flight bypasses all of that and takes you into immediate action without thinking. After you have taken your time, and you are alone, take a paper or a journal, and go through these steps of the empowerment process. You can also call a buddy to go through this with you.

1. Write down what you are angry about. You can recall other times when you felt angry in the same way, and express yourself in as complete and uninhibited a way as possible. No one is going to be affected by it or hurt by it. Express yourself without any repression. Ask yourself:

   What made me angry?

   Why did I feel angry?

   When else have I felt angry in a similar way?

   What is it that I want?

2. Take some time to wait for the answers to come. The more you shift from being angry to recognizing what you want to create for yourself and others, you will feel more energy flowing, and the anger will dissipate. The anger was the frustration of not getting the outcome you wanted. Keep dropping to deeper levels, allowing destructive

desires to morph into positive ones: "I hate them... I want to quit... I want them all to go away... I want peace... I want to be respected... I want my gifts to be seen... I want to give my gifts..."

3. Now drop deeper to a sense of deserving.

> *What is it about my intention that is reasonable?*
>
> *What do I deserve to have? What do others deserve to have?*
>
> *What is it that is good for me and others to have?*

4. Now drop into a sense of "Yes I can have that. We can have that." This increases your confidence and ability to take leadership.

This process will shift you from anger to constructive action and will also build others' trust in you.

Celebrate Pure Energy

When you are really angry, it also makes you feel very alive. When you step away from the situation, and go away on your own, you can discover that you have a lot of energy in your body. Sometimes it can be very helpful just to let that energy move.

Arjuna says: There was a time in my life when I had shut down any possibility of getting angry. I had become a wimp. I found ways to get friendly with my primal power, and it helped me a lot. You can growl, you can beat a cushion, or you can hit a punching bag. The idea is not exactly to get something out, as though you are doing some sort of colonic. Instead, the idea is just to come alive with it and to enjoy it. You are celebrating your aliveness. To get good at this, you have to completely let go of the story by exploring your body.

Anger explodes through the top of your head and fills you with light. You can think of it like a thermometer. When you are caught up in the story, the story keeps the temperature at about 50 degrees. If you let go of the story and increase the anger without any story, you can push the liquid in the thermometer up to the 70 degree mark. If you can increase it even more (some people even like to have a baseball bat and a cushion in their room, so they can go crazy), you can push the liquid in the thermometer up to the 90 degree line. If you push through even more and forget everything about why you are angry, you can fully enter into anger for the enjoyment of it. Then you can cause the liquid to burst through the top of the thermometer and to cascade down the sides. If you can allow energy to explode in this way, close your eyes and notice that you are now completely full of light. That is a wonderful way to allow anger to fully move through you so that it becomes light and love. It is a completely non-cerebral process.

Learn from Remorse

Another great practice to do when you feel really angry is to be alone and remember a time when you acted on this anger. Go back and remember a time in the past when you gave this anger free reign, and remember what happened. What did you say? What did you do? Maybe you broke something. Maybe there were even times you hit someone in anger. Because it is not happening now, because it is a memory, you can remember the consequence. If you hit someone, you can remember how he reacted. Maybe that person became afraid of you and cut you off. Maybe you lost that person's trust permanently. If you broke something, remember how you felt about that later when you calmed down. Remorse can be a great teacher when it turns a destructive force into a valuable lesson. By connecting the anger now to your remorse in memory, you feel the consequence of acting on anger, and that will allow you to be present with your anger without having to act it out.

Practice Forgiveness

Once you open the channel of remorse, you will naturally have more of a sense of your own hurt and vulnerability, so you will also be able to feel other people's feelings. You can ask yourself, based on what this person has said and done, *What are they feeling that has caused them to behave in this way?*

1. Put two cushions on the floor.

2. Sit on one of the cushions, close your eyes, and imagine the other person in front of you. Let yourself get really angry at the person. Allow yourself to fully experience your anger, and express it.

3. Shift cushions, and experiment to see if you can experience what the other person is feeling. Enter into what is going on in this other person, what the emotional state is that is causing this person to be frustrated, to be angry, to be blaming, and to be attacking.

4. Come back to your cushion, and feel what it is like now.

5. Simply by moving backwards and forwards from feeling and expressing your own feelings to becoming the other person on the other cushion, the anger will turn into compassion, into an increased capacity to see things from both perspectives. This is great leadership.

Practice Appreciation

When you feel angry, take some time out, and after the anger has dissipated, think about all the positive things this other person has done for you and why he or she does them. It is because they want to support you in some way. You can seek out their positive intention. What is this person's greatest priority? What is the greatest intent in their life? When we are left to automatic thinking, we tend to just look at red lights instead of realizing how many green lights we have.

John says: One day I was driving through Mill Valley, and my daughter said to me, "Daddy, why are the lights always red? It seems like we're always stopping at the red light. Why don't we get green lights?"

So I said, "Lauren, let's do an experiment. Let's drive around town and count how many green lights we get versus how many red lights we get." We drove around the town, and we discovered that we had three times more green lights than red lights. And yet it seemed like we were only getting red lights because when you get a red light, you are stuck for a long time, but when you get a green light, you just flow through. In just the same way, when you get frustrated with your partner, after the initial tension has dissipated, think about how many green lights your partner gives you versus the very few red lights in contrast.

When Someone Is Angry with You

If someone gets really angry with you, whether it is your partner, a family member, or a co-worker, and for some reason it is impossible to take space to go and feel, you could stay present and consciously step into the energy of their anger. It is a good idea if you have already done some practice with getting more grounded in your body as we explained in earlier chapters. When someone is really angry, sink your weight a little bit by bending your knees slightly so that you bring your pelvis just an inch or so closer to the ground. But do this subtly enough that the other person does not burst out laughing! Breathe, and if necessary, just bring your hands to the lower part of your belly so you feel your center of gravity coming lower. Look into this person's eyes, and before you say anything in response to the anger, be present and take the tiniest step forward. Just half an inch is enough. Stepping into the anger is a way to communicate, "I'm right here" or "I am listening to what you are saying." This will not only cause the other person's anger to dissipate, but it will also shift you from reactive anger to becoming present. And this will allow you to return more to yourself and to earn more trust as a leader.

FOR WOMEN

Everyone gets angry. We all get impatient, frustrated, and sometimes lose our cool. Although we all love our partners, there are times when anger takes us over so completely that we react without any awareness of how we sound.

Men particularly have little awareness of how scary it can be to a woman when he gets angry. Throughout history, in more primitive times, when men got angry, someone was often hurt or killed. When a woman was angry, a man only got the cold shoulder and not a death sentence. This distinction has many consequences in an intimate relationships. When a man gets angry, he is generally unconscious of how and why he shuts a woman down. He reasons that if she is angry, he can be just as angry. This may seem fair, but it is not.

If you are together with a man who aspires to be conscious and who has been practicing—as we hope you are—he will be able to catch the moment before he does anything that he will later regret, and he will be able to say, "I need to take space. I need to get away now. I need to digest what you are saying. Give me some time." That is the best thing for a man to do. It also builds his capacity to take leadership and gain your and others' respect.

If he says this, it is important not to go after him. Anger will dissipate once a man gets space. Men have natural mechanisms within them to digest what is going on. Eventually, a good man will come to see his side and will come back with a greater understanding and ability to listen.

If you do live with a man whose anger does sometimes get out of control, and even erupts into physical violence, please do not stay isolated and alone with that. Make sure that everyone who is close to you and loves you knows what is happening. If a man has trouble managing his anger, you are not protecting him by keeping it a secret. You are endangering yourself and potentially cutting him off from getting help. All men feel anger, and there is nothing wrong with it. But not all men know how to channel their anger responsibly. If your man has not learned that yet, trust that he is teachable and trainable and that with the right support, he can become the man you trust and feel safe with.

Finally, if you are single, we would like to suggest that there are three different kinds of men, with respect to anger, to whom you can feel attracted. One is the angry and sometimes violent man. He gets into conflicts quickly; he may have a history of violence with previous partners. If you know that a part of you gets attracted to that kind of man, it may be left over from an association of love with anger from your past, even with your father. In this case, talk to your friends and even to a therapist, and ask your friends to vet potential partners before you get too involved.

The second kind of man is one who never feels anger or even irritation. He smiles, speaks in a calm, low voice, and exudes only love and peace. He claims to never feel anger or to have gone beyond it completely through some kind of spiritual practice. Some women feel attracted to such a man because of a fear, also left over from the past, of even a whiff of male power and what it might lead to. You might also think twice about such a man. Over time, we have noticed that it can be hard for a woman to sustain respect for such a man.

The third kind of man can feel anger. He can assert authority and does not back down in fear of confrontation. He takes a bold stand in the face of injustice or wrongdoing. No one walks over him, and he does not hesitate to protect you and defend you. But he is aware and conscious. His emotions do not get out of control or eclipse his better judgment. He is a natural leader, and people respect his decisions. Such a man is the one we wish for you.

A Conscious Man:

ROB ALLBEE, FOUNDER OF THE INSIDE CIRCLE

A huge part of my work has been dealing with anger, with rage. My father regularly beat me as a child. I grew up in violence. I thought all kids were treated like that. By the time I was seventeen, I had already been in and out of institutions, got busted for car theft, burglaries, and other things. My best friend, Ramone, and I got caught committing a commercial burglary. The police came, but we ran. They chased us in their car down an alley. It was 4:00 a.m. At the end of the alley, I ran to the left and Ramone ran to the right. I could hear the gunshots as I got away. The next day they came to arrest me. They told me they had shot Ramone dead, that I would go to prison for his death under the felony murder rule.

They showed me a picture. He was lying face down on the ground with a huge gunshot wound in his back. I could see his face. We had been really close—we'd ridden motorcycles together down the coast, told each other our life stories, and the places where we hurt. We shared everything with each other, but there he was on the ground—dead.

I could feel some piece of me breaking, a snapping inside. Every last, little bit of *I'm going to try to do better, I'm going try to figure what this is all about,* disappeared. I just gave up; I didn't care any more. When I got out of prison I started shooting heroin. It was the only thing that I could find that was strong enough to pour water on that fire. All that mattered was getting revenge and taking my anger out on world. I hated cops. I hated anyone in a uniform, really, no matter if it was a mailman or an airline pilot. I wanted to kill everyone that wore a uniform.

I had three sons with three different women. I was not part of my two older boys' lives because I was still running amuck. When my youngest son was born, I realized it was my last chance. If I was seriously going to take on the idea of being a dad, and being there for this little guy, I had to find a way.

I met a number of men who were involved in men's work and I was invited to participate in some men's circles. When I began to examine my emotions, I found that if I gave them a chance to speak it was typically very clear what they were trying to say. I began to see emotions as tools to inform me of what was happening in my life. I understand now that anger is a response we have when something really big needs to get done. It is informing us that we may be experiencing some form of injustice, some breach of our boundaries.

The first time I was invited to examine my anger in a men's group I thought, *You guys are nuts.* "I'm starting to get pissed," I told them. A man there said, "Good, let yourself just be pissed." "If I get pissed, I'm gonna break everything in this fucking room. I'm gonna hurt people." "No, you're not," they said. I was willing to trust them, and they were capable of being there in a way that allowed me to feel for the first time. You've got to let people get close, and that is hard. You have to hold them sometimes, too.

I had to find out, *What am I trying to protect? What is being insulted or invaded? Where is the attack coming from?* Most often, when I could let go of the idea of an outside attack, I would discover what part of me was feeling attacked. Underneath, there was the same old thing: the part of me that felt I did not matter. That part of me was getting hurt again and again, in a deep way. *Don't you see that is what I'm feeling?* But no one ever did—all they saw was my rage. And I took it out on everybody around me.

One day I went to a talk by Malidoma Patrice Somé, a writer and teacher from Africa. At the end of the talk, he walked all the way to the back where I was sitting, and said "Here's my card, call me. We've got work to do." The next week I called him.

He talked about how the Dagara people treat each other where he is from. They know that each person is uniquely valuable to the overall well being of the entire community. This concept touched me deeply. He told me stories of how the children are named and how they are each given a unique song. When the children do something wrong, they are not punished; instead the community sings them their song to remind them of their gift, their essence. They say there that someone can only harm another, or do something wrong, when they have somehow forgotten who they really are. That made perfect sense to me.

He invited me to his village in Burkina Faso and I ended up spending a lot of time there over the next years. In his community, each person's individual manifestation of the sacred is seen as crucial to the overall well being of the village, so the loss of one piece affects everybody.

When I was there, he introduced me to his medicine man. I had always felt responsible for Ramone's death. The medicine man told me, "You knew who Ramone was, didn't you? You knew what his gift was." I said I did. "Part of your responsibility, then, is to bring Ramone's song, his gift to your community, to your family and friends," the medicine man said. "You also have the responsibility to bring your own medicine and make it available, but now you also have this added task to make sure Ramone's medicine does not go to waste. Can you bring the gift of who he was to the world?"

This gave me something tangible to work on. But how would I bring the gift of who Ramone was to the world?

Ramone was a fun, adventurous guy, full of laughter. How could I discover my own gift and song, but also be available for his as well? I wasn't sure, but it was the only thing I felt I could do to alleviate my feeling of responsibility for the death of another human being. That was the thing that made the shift.

When the opportunity first came up to do outreach in prisons, I was hesitant. But I did it, in part because I had the feeling Ramone would have—he had the kind of charisma to go into prisons and make himself available. I would not have done it on my own, but I was motivated to share Ramone's song, and so his essence became a real part of my life.

When I talk to men in prison, I tell them my own story and how I am singing Ramone's song for him. Then I ask the men if they have been responsible for someone else's death, and if they could also find a way to do the same thing I am doing for Ramone. For many men, this is the turning point.

Chapter Seven

HE STANDS BY HIS BROTHER

A Conscious Man forms deep, sustainable relationships with other men in a way that supports them both to deepen their masculinity. For most men, a few very deep friendships will be all that they need. In fact, for some men, just having one best friend will completely fulfill his needs for friendship in a way that nourishes and sustains him. When a man finds another man, or men, to bond with in this way, it feels like his family. Hence, even when there is no biological connection, the man will refer to a close friend as his "brother."

There is a huge range of what men can bring out in each other when they meet. Men can easily get together and support each other to be less conscious, more superficial, and more distracted. Equally, once they understand what is required, men can support each other in depth, awareness, and focus on their true mission.

The way that men support each other is quite different from what happens when women get together. Women can be happy to meet each other, to not do anything special, but just to talk. Sharing feelings and stories from the day and empathizing with problems all support women to relax and deepen together. For men, it is quite different. Generally, men bring out the best in each other and give each other the greatest support when they get together around a specific focus. One good way this can happen is around getting something done, a shared sense of a goal to accomplish. So when men help each other out building a shed, writing a book together, doing business, partaking in activism, or achieving any other project that is working towards a fixed outcome, it becomes a context in which they bring out the best in each other and also feel a sense of bonding and brotherhood.

Another way this can happen is by forming a mastermind group. Although these could be equally for men and women, it is another great way for men to support each other. A mastermind group generally meets regularly and is an opportunity for men to support each other around their goals, work, and sense of mission. Each man in the circle can compare challenges he is facing with what he wants to accomplish and request feedback and insights from other men.

Form a Men's Group

Many men also greatly benefit from forming a "men's group" that meets regularly. Now the purpose of the gathering is not just around work and mission, but it becomes a broader context for men to bond and to support each other to be the best they can be. That is how we came to write this book. We have been part of the same men's group for many years now. The group meets in Marin County, just north of San Francisco, and Arjuna lives several hours away in the Sierra Nevada Mountains. It is a long drive home, so one month, he sent an email asking if someone could put him up for the night. John offered. After the group meeting was over, we went back to John's house together, and we had a cup of tea. It was about 10 o'clock. We started to talk about the group, and then more generally about men's groups, and then more generally about what it means to be a man in today's world. The next time we looked at the clock, it was 2:30 in the morning. The next month, this happened again, and then again, and so we realized we were sharing some great insights in these conversations. We started to record them, and this book is the result.

We have already talked in this book about the ways that a Conscious Man can experience feelings, and the chaos of his life, in a bigger space of awareness. He is able to contain his shifting thoughts and feelings within a larger context. A men's group offers exactly the same kind of a container. It allows a man to express what is going on with him and for it to be contained within the bigger space of other men, who are listening and who can also offer insight when invited. Now the whole integrated brain is created not just within one man but within a gathering of men. When a man talks about his challenges, he can move into the primitive reptilian brain (fight or flight) or into the feeling part of the brain. The other men who are listening, holding space, and remaining conscious and present, move into the pre-frontal cortex. It means that you can sit in the circle, you can relax and allow yourself to be as you are, and you can be heard and witnessed by a group of conscious friends.

It is a very different experience for a man than talking with a woman or in mixed company. You have to try it out to realize just how different it is. When you are with your woman, or in mixed company, you are a man, and your experience is not the same as a woman's. You never quite know: "Is this normal what I'm feeling and thinking? I don't feel the same as she does, or in fact the way her friends do. Is there something wrong with me?"

This kind of insecurity can easily lead you to edit what you are thinking and feeling. It may seem too gross, too crude, too driven, too ambitious, or too competitive. When you are with a group of men, it allows you to experience the universality of the masculine experience.

When you meet with other men in a structured way and listen to each other, it allows you to become aware of your experience. It allows you to listen to what other men are experiencing, and naturally, everyone present becomes more aware of themselves, more accepting of themselves. Thus, a deepening happens on its own. Men are not always aware of what is going on inside them, and they do not always know how to articulate it because we are more action oriented. When another man can speak about what is happening for him, it also clarifies it for you: "Yes... I have that experience too." It gives you objectivity so that you can see your own pain, or confusion, over there on the other side of the circle reflected back to you. And so you come to understand yourself, and masculinity in general, more clearly. "I never thought about it before. I just assumed this was my thing and I was alone with it. But he's got the same thing going on too, and he's a pretty conscious guy." Meeting in a men's group on a regular basis in this way does not need to be about giving advice unless it is asked for. Men can hold each other accountable to their highest potential, to their deepest intention, but always in an atmosphere of acceptance and being conscious.

One great example of this is that men instinctively think about sex and notice beautiful women around them all the time. Research tells that us the average man, walking down the street, will experience a fleeting feeling of attraction to a beautiful woman at least once a minute. Women do not experience the same thing. If a man was to talk honestly about these fleeting superficial attractions that pass through his mind all the time with his wife or with their friends, she would not feel okay about it. So he does not admit to being the way that he is in front of his wife. He may go through years of noticing other women in this way and thinking that something is wrong with him. The benefit of a man being with other men is that he can say, "I notice beautiful women all the time. It's like an obsession." Another man then can say, "I do also, brother, and so do we all. It's a guy thing. Do you act on it? No. Then there's nothing wrong with that. It's biology." This is just one random example: fleeting attraction. But there are hundreds of things like that, which a man will not admit to with women present, and he will hardly even admit it to himself.

Being romantic can increase your feminine hormones, while being with other men will balance that. When you are with your woman, you do many things together, but always in the back of your mind, you may be wondering when you will have sex again. To do that, you have to prepare for it, which involves a very elaborate and often extended process of foreplay. You have to jump through hoops. You have to listen. You have to be romantic. You have to be affectionate. You have to be understanding. You have to be patient. You need to slow down. You have to soften. You have to do all this and more to be able to get anywhere close to her vagina. To do all these things, you have to tune into your sensitive side. At a certain point, when you are making too much estrogen and not enough testosterone, you need to come back into balance. That is the time to go hang out with your male friends and support each other in being men.

Structure

There are two important differences between how men meet together and how women meet together. Understanding these will allow you to make the best use of your time when you meet with other men in a way that can most benefit everybody. The first has to do with structure. When women meet together, they do not really need any structure. They can just hang out, enjoy some good food, talk, and laugh spontaneously, and they will automatically relax more deeply into being more feminine, more relaxed, and letting go of stress. If men meet together without structure, they are more likely to gravitate towards the most superficial common denominator. Men just hanging out without any agenda is more likely to bring out the most shallow aspects of each man rather than the depth. You may end up chatting about football scores, car engines, or politics. It may be a fun time but not necessarily deepening. Structure allows you to gravitate towards depth, presence, and a shared sense of purpose.

An example of structure would be when a man speaks for three minutes about how he is challenged. Then we go around the circle, and each man has exactly one minute to give precise and concise feedback and suggestions. Starting a gathering with ten minutes of silence, or abstaining from alcohol or other substances before and during the meeting, are other examples of structure. As soon as you determine and follow structured agreements, the meeting goes deeper, and you discover your masculine essence more fully.

Challenge

The second important difference has to do with challenge and support. When women get together, they bring out the best in each other by supporting, loving, and appreciating: "You are beautiful, you have so much to give, and you do so much for everybody." If that were all that men did together when they met, it would leave something missing. Men bring out the best in each other by also adding an element of challenge: by calling each other forth to their higher potential. Sometimes, a man can support another man by pointing out inconsistencies in what he is saying or reminding him of intentions he has stated in the past that he is not fully living now. All of this happens in a bigger context of acceptance, friendship, and support. But the acceptance now has an evolutionary edge to it. It means there is a polarity between what is happening today, your intuition of your fullest potential, and what you are pulled towards. Evolution happens in that tension between acceptance of what is here now and awareness of the highest possibility.

For example, in our men's group, one man was having challenges with his marriage. He was feeling hopeless and thinking about leaving his wife. Then another man might say, "I hear that you're overwhelmed by this situation. But think about what you are doing. You've got kids. Is this what you really want? Is this what you really stand for?" There is acceptance of the difficulties of the situation, acceptance of the feeling of wanting to give up, but there is also an even deeper acceptance of your potential, of your highest intention, of the promises you have made in the past.

WHAT GETS IN THE WAY

Homophobic Harry

One of the strongest reasons that men do not form deeper bonds with other men, particularly in the U.S., is because of a collective fear of being gay. The fear of being seen as homosexual, labeled as homosexual, or actually being homosexual, remains extraordinarily strong despite all of the advances we have seen in the last decades towards accepting different sexual preferences.

Arjuna says: I remember a couple of years ago I went on a camping trip with a good friend. He was something like a brother from another mother.

When we got into the Trinity Alps, far away from anywhere, it was pouring rain. The thought of hiking for hours through the rain and then setting up a tent seemed to be unnecessarily masochistic. So instead we went to the small historic town of Weaverville to find a hotel. The only place we could find was a motel that had one room left. With one queen-sized bed. We looked at each other for a moment, laughed, and said, "Okay, we'll take it." The woman behind the counter started to talk to us, assuming we were a gay couple. So we explained to her that we were both married but taking this camping trip together. She then expressed amazement with a tinge of admiration. She told us that in a situation like this, she had experienced that women would have no trouble sharing a bed together, but she had almost never seen two men willing to share a bed unless they were in a gay relationship.

Why are so many men afraid that they might be seen as gay even if they are heterosexual? Of course, this is partly a vestige from times past, not that long ago, when homosexuality was viewed as immoral and illegal. Many men fear being feminized and they associate being feminized with being homosexual, even though this is a very inaccurate stereotype. Furthermore, the black and white distinction between "gay" and "straight" has been also exposed as inaccurate, as we discover that many men can, at different times in their lives, feel attraction for both men and women.

To be able to deeply explore and get benefits from your connection with other men, you have to be willing to face your prejudices against homosexuality, and your fears of being gay, and get over them. If you are gay or bisexual, accept it and enjoy it. If you are heterosexual, relax and let go of needless nervousness. The bond that you can then create with other men is a form of love just as powerful and important as the love you feel with your intimate partner, with your children, and with your parents. Then your connection with other men is not just about creating work projects. You value each other, you miss each other, and you can rely upon each other. To your wife, you can say, "I love you, honey." To your best friend, you can say, "I love you, bro."

Competitive Colin

Perhaps you remember the great film *Stand by Me* about three young boys growing up together in the 1950s. It is the year before they enter into adolescence. At the beginning of the film, the writer is going back to his hometown for a funeral, and he remembers those days: "I never had any friends later on like the ones I had when I was twelve. Jesus, does anyone?" It is a beautiful film, particularly for men to see, because it reminds us of that time before puberty when friendships with other boys were deep and uncomplicated. There is a closeness you have with your brothers, with other boys, that gets lost when you enter into puberty and an element of competition sets in. Once we enter puberty, testosterone levels dramatically rise, and we get interested for the first time in girls. We have to figure out how to impress them if we want their attention. When you first feel arousal, it is like a drug has hit you. It has tremendous power, and suddenly all your focus shifts to what it takes to make girls happy. If you want to get the girl, you need to compete with the guy next to you, and you need to be better than him and more impressive than him. There is only one prize here: only one of you will win her.

Until we become aware of it, our urge to impress in adolescence can initiate a mad rush to succeed and perform that can last the rest of your life. When the striving for success eclipses everything else, your relationships with other men become utilitarian. How can he help me get ahead? How can I use him as part of my business plan? Is this relationship strategic? It is all part of the pressure to succeed at all costs. The way to balance this mad rush to success, and use other men as part of that process, is to recognize the value of friendship in your life. It has a benefit to you independent of how the friendship helps you with your professional goals.

Negligent Nigel

All relationships at some point require maintenance. They require apologies, clearing up of misunderstandings, and reaffirming commitments. In your marriage, you sometimes need to put work into it. You might even sometimes need to go to counseling. With your kids, you know that you need to put work into them too, and it would not be unusual to go to a family therapist to work on that as well. At work, conflicts are taken seriously, and it would not be unusual to speak with a mediator when you are not getting along with a co-worker. But almost all men would shy away from giving the same kind of attention to a friendship with another man. Why should a friendship between two men be any different? It still needs maintenance to stay current and healthy. Consequently, men often think of their friends as more replaceable than their intimate partner, family members, or even the people they work with. Because we do not always know how to nurture and repair friendships when they go off track, we cut off our friends over small misunderstandings instead of staying present and moving through the more difficult process of apology and forgiveness.

THE PRACTICES

Join or Create a Men's Group.

We have been part of the same men's group for many years. Besides our marriages and families, these are definitely the most important relationships in our lives. We meet in a structured way once a month, and once or twice a year we go away together to John's ranch for a retreat. But it spills way beyond the structured meetings. For birthdays, at Christmas time, and on Oscar night, these are the friendships that we built and deepen over many years and that nurture us both in so many ways. It is so invaluable, so important, and such an unparalleled catalyst to becoming an awake and mature man, that we would recommend every man on the planet to make this practice a part of their lives.

One good way to find a men's group is to participate in the Mankind Project's New Warrior Initiation weekend, which is held around the world regularly. Once you go through the weekend, you can join an "i-group" and have a group of men to meet with regularly. Or there are many other groups that meet without being aligned to any particular organization. If you cannot find such a group in your area, gather together the men you feel closest to, and create your own group.

The key to a successful men's group is structure. If you just get together to hang out, break open a six-pack, and talk about whatever comes into your head, it may be a fun evening, but it does not offer the same benefits. As soon as men meet together in a structured way, it automatically brings greater depth, honesty, and a return to being conscious and aware of your mission. Choose men to meet with where you can see the possibility of supporting each other to live at your highest potentials. The more that each man in the group has some sense of mission, the more powerful the group will be.

Once you gather your men, you will be able to decide together on the structure that works best for you. We both recommend that the group should have a rotating leadership: each time you meet, a different man leads the group. Having one fixed leader will probably create less benefit both for the leader and for the other men involved: it re-creates a sense of hierarchy out of which we are now evolving. Ten to twelve men is an ideal number for a good group. Two to three hours, once a week to once a month, is the time you will need.

He is a suggested structure you could play with:

Start the group at a fixed time. Emphasize the importance of being on time, and if a man is late, it would be a good opportunity to focus together on the importance of keeping your word. You can begin with **a few minutes of silence** together. In our group, we close our eyes. Depending upon your background, this could be a time of meditation, reflection, or prayer.

Check-in. Start the group with a check-in round. Each man takes a few minutes to briefly speak of what is going on in his life. It is important during this round that there is no interruption, no feedback, and no cracking jokes. During this check-in phase, you will sense if anyone in the group is having trouble and needs support from the group.

Support. Not everybody needs support every week but often just one or two people do. This might be a relationship difficulty, a challenge with money or work, concerning news about health, or any unresolved challenge. The man who needs support takes five minutes to speak, again uninterrupted, about what is challenging him. Use a timer, which helps a man to discipline himself to stay focused and get to the point.

When this man has finished describing his challenge, go around the circle with each man providing empathy, insight, or suggestions for one minute each. There should be no backward and forward discussion.

Once every man has spoken, it comes back again to the man who requested help. He now gets another two minutes to reflect upon what he has received.

Guided activities. Once every man who needs support has received in this way, you can use the rest of your time together in some form of guided activity, which should be led by the man whose turn it is to lead that night. We sometimes will open with a topic to talk about together. It might be sexuality, money, fatherhood, or aging. When we do this, it is also done in a structured way. Someone will propose a topic, and then we go around the circle with each man speaking about this for two or three minutes each. This may sound to you to be very rigid. But it works. We have each been part of men's groups for decades, and in every case, we have discovered that open-ended, unstructured discussion can be interesting and fun, but does not bring this deepening of masculine presence in the way that a structured meeting does.

Create Structured Friendships

If you have a men's group, you can also spend one-on-one time with specific men in the group. If you are not part of a men's group, think of the men you already feel closest to or those whom you would like to get to know better. Experiment spending time together one-on-one in a way that consciously and deliberately deepens your conscious masculine presence. These kind of meetings can often be tied to doing something together: playing tennis or other sports, hiking, or making music.

The way that you can bring structure to friendship is quite similar to what we described above in a group. One man can take 5 or 10 minutes to describe something difficult or challenging for him. Then the other man can take 5 or 10 minutes to offer reflection or advice. Another way you can deepen together is to take five minutes each to say to the other man certain comments:

"This is where I see you are holding yourself back from your fullest potential."

"Something I don't think you see about yourself is..."

"The greatest contribution I feel you have to make is..."

"The thing I see people most admire about you is..."

If you take 15 to 20 minutes to practice together in this way, you can then drop the structure, and the depth will remain. These kinds of questions will allow you to change gears together. Once you have hit the mother lode — man supporting man, each in his depth and remembering his values and purpose — then later, if you continue talking in an unstructured way, that depth will be maintained. Now break open a six pack and any small illegalities you enjoy, and let it rip.

When you meet with another man in this way, you need to have overt permission before you give feedback or offer support. Otherwise, it will feel invasive and will create conflict between yourselves. If you use the kind of structured sentences described above, the permission is obvious. If you feel you have something important to contribute to a man as feedback or advice, ask him first, "Are you open to suggestions or feedback?"

Challenges

Men bring out the best in each other through challenges but always within a bigger context of acceptance and support. So a great way to deepen your friendship with another man, in a way that you can palpably feel the support you have for each other, is to offer each other challenges to be completed within a specific time frame. A challenge needs to follow certain guidelines:

1. It needs to be very clearly defined what the successful completion of the challenge would look like. So "Be more friendly to people," would be hard to clearly define. But "Call your brother, whom you have not spoken to for three months, and tell him what you appreciate about him," is something that can be checked off as done or not done in an unambiguous way.

2. Both men need to be completely on board with the challenge. If either one has any objection that it is too difficult, illegal, immoral, or would harm anyone in any way, that needs to be respected.

Here are a few examples:

Sit silently for 10 minutes when you get home from work before you move into family time.
Stop drinking alcohol for a week.
Take your wife out to dinner and the theater on a Thursday night.
Call your father and tell him how much you appreciate all he has given to you.
Get down on the floor and play with your kids for at least 10 minutes when you get home.

FOR WOMEN

When men get together with other men, they do it in a very different way than how you spend time with other women. This may require him to edit himself when he is with you. The way men talk sometimes with other men you would probably find rude, crude, or abrasive. Some of the things men say in jest to other men you might even consider to be cruel or unkind.

Men need time with other men to relax and be themselves. When your man wants that, let him go. Sometimes he needs to pull away from you in order to come back refreshed, interested in meeting and missing you, and wanting to bring something of himself to you.

Think of living with a man as comparable to having a big dog in the house. The dog probably loves you a lot and quickly learns how to behave in the house. When you say "Sit," the dog sits and waits. A dog that loves you will behave well and not get on the furniture if you don't want him to. But as you know, every now and then, you have to take the dog to the park. Then the dog will run like crazy, and sniff at the asses of other dogs, and bark and play rough with the dogs. If you can let the dog off the leash at the park now and then, you'll have a happy dog, and your dog will behave well when you bring him in the house again. Of course, being a man is not the same as being a dog. You are dealing with a different species. But still, you are living with an animal who is very different from you. Just like the dog, we are happy to be polite and well behaved and clean up after ourselves, but we need some time when we can just be raw and unedited with other men.

There are lots of things men like to talk about with other men that would bore you to death. Men get interested in engines, how things are built, football scores, and sometimes obscure facts and details that can be boring to the feminine mind. In just the same way, you know that there are many things that interest you and your friends that can be boring to men. You have conversations with your friends you would never have with a man there because you would not feel comfortable. You would feel like you have to translate and explain. That is why it is so important for you to have time with your women friends and for him to have time with other men.

We have noticed that women can have three reactions, broadly speaking, to a man wanting to spend time with other men. The first is resentment and the feeling that a man being with other men is taking time away from you. When you feel that way, you can make a date to have quality time together soon, after he has had time with the guys.

The second reaction we have noticed women have to men being with other men is to think that men should be more relational: "Why don't you call Peter; why don't you call David, and go do something together?" Sometimes women feel that men should be closer with other men in just the same way that women are close with other women. But it does not always work like that. Men develop relationships with men in a different way than you develop relationships with women. Please don't try and organize a man into developing deeper friendships. Just let him go and do things his own way when he wants to go.

The third response women sometimes have to men being with other men is to offer insights about how to deepen relationships and harmonize. This can be really useful to your man. On the whole, women understand better than men how to create sustainable relationships. Women tend to have a better sense of when it is time to visit someone who is sick, or send a thank you note, or to offer help and support even when it has not been requested.

When there is a conflict with another man, men do not always know what to do about it, and the friendship drifts apart and becomes more distant. Those are times when you can support a man and remind him of the value of friendship. However, before you give advice, it is best to ask if it is welcome. If it is, it becomes a way you can support your man to make good decisions about relationships.

A CONSCIOUS MAN:

KEN DRUCK, AUTHOR OF THE SECRETS MEN KEEP

I was blessed with a wonderful friendship early in my life when I moved to Colorado and met an extraordinary man named Terry. We were both young fathers working in the mental health field. We both loved to play and enjoy ourselves, to trek into the mountains. When the walls of fear started coming down there was a world of discovery about what it truly meant to love another man: an adopted, spiritual brother. We listened to one another talk about the challenges and the pains and the setbacks and the fears and the failures of being a father, as well as the joys. We talked about doing the work that we were doing, about being guys, about loving sports. All those things allowed us to drop down into conversations I'd never had with another man.

The intimacy that flowed from this relationship taught me that one of the greatest wastes of this life is when we miss out on the brotherhood that's waiting there for us with other men. We get to learn from one another, to transcend the shame and self-consciousness or the fear of failure—whatever it is that's holding us back. We can compete fiercely, but then we can laugh about it, laugh at ourselves and learn and love one another.

I learned what it meant to love another man from my relationship with Terry. He and I were clearly heterosexual, but we discovered the joy of hugging each other, the feel of being held in the arms of a strong, trusting, loving, caring brother. We were not going to hold back from the richness of a friendship that opened both of our eyes and hearts.

My relationship with Terry provided me with the template for everything I've ever come to understand about what true friendship is between men.

It wasn't only successes. We went through hardships and real challenging periods. He eventually went through a divorce and moved out of the area; later he remarried. Then he called me one day and said that he had been diagnosed with terminal cancer. The final chapter in our friendship was me helping my best friend die. We decided to take a trip and meet up in northern California. This was going to be our time together. I remember walking on the beach, arm in arm, crying together, and laughing hysterically together with the most beautiful, sacred connection.

His kids and my kids got to witness what it looks like when men love each other. In a world where guys live at arm's length, so few men have deep friendships, not just golfing buddies. So few men have friends who know their souls, who know them beyond their stories, and know what makes their hearts sing.

I was with Terry three days before he died. I've never had to do anything more difficult in my life than to say goodbye to my best friend. He was so weak that I had to carry him when he wanted to move to the next room. He was too weak to shower, but on the day I left, he decided he wanted one last one. I told him I would wash him. I carried him to the bathroom and gave my friend a shower. I love him, and washing him was one of greatest honors. "Kenny, we did good," he said. "We have fought, and we have disagreed about men's issues, and hundreds of other issues. But we have gone through a great journey together." He was blessing it all. He was blessing the entirety of it. And I still carry this blessing with me today.

Chapter Eight

HE KEEPS HIS WORD

In order for a man to feel motivated and to achieve and accomplish his soul's mission, he needs to be able to make promises that he can keep. When a man feels that life is too easy, he does not grow. The power of keeping your word is that every time you do your very best to follow through on actions, when you do not feel like it but you do it anyway, it realigns you to your deepest openness and clarity: who you were at the time when you made the promise. Sometimes you may need to change a promise if it no longer serves everyone, but regularly making and keeping promises continuously binds you back to your deepest integrity and to your most open heart.

John says: I often work with men who feel they have not accomplished enough or feel they have failed. When I ask them why they take certain actions, or say certain things, I hear the response, "I just felt like it." Following feelings is fine, but you also need the part of you that can be analytical and can ask, "Why am I doing this? What are the things that

I want to accomplish and achieve in the long term?" This often means choosing long-term satisfaction over short-term pleasure.

Our ancestors, driven by the hyper-masculine trance, did what they did because they had been given a particular role. A man was given goals, and he would then make promises based on what was expected of him. He got married, got a job, and knew exactly what to do to be a real man. It was done in obedience to what the culture defined for us. This worked at the time because he could predict the environment and make promises that were possible to keep. Sometimes these would be fulfilled over decades. Today, the environment is changing so fast, in technology, at work, in relationships and in many other ways, so deciding on a course and sticking to it no matter what is often no longer possible.

Starting in the 1960s, men began to rebel against having choices defined for them from birth. They wanted to listen to what was in their hearts: "I want to choose my own life rather than my culture, my family, my tradition, making these choices for me." As a reaction to the rigidity of the 1950s, men learned to follow their feelings and go with the flow. This meant that men were leaning more into their feminine side, which is more influenced by estrogen. Instead of sacrificing immediate pleasure to achieve goals, men grew more sensitive to what feels good in the moment. Running on fleeting feelings can bring you down as a man, because when you start to feel from your heart, you may find fears and fleeting desires which can constantly distract you and then cause you to feel untrustworthy.

A New Integration

The Conscious Man learns to balance his masculine and feminine sides, which allows him to have awareness of his higher purpose in life in a way that is also sensitive to the changing environment in which he is moving. He is aware of his emotions, but he also maintains the ability to do the right thing, even when he is afraid. He may set a goal and later realize that it was not a good goal if the promise no longer serves him or anyone else. Then, through his feeling and intuition, he can adjust his course, set new goals, and make new promises based on new information.

For example, in the past, many people stuck it out in marriages long after they were only causing everyone to suffer. Men stayed in jobs they hated because they were tough men. An overly feminized man might move from partner to partner, seeking out new pleasurable romantic feelings, or move from one job to another in following his bliss. A Conscious Man can make these promises intelligently: he can ride the ups and downs of marriage and face the trials and defeats of his job, but he also knows when to quit in the service of everyone's wellbeing.

Crossing Things off on Lists

Making short-term promises, to himself and to others, that are in alignment with his long-term vision is incredibly important for a Conscious Man to stay healthy. He can push through difficulties and challenges because of adequate levels of testosterone in his blood. When he reaches a milestone, which can be something small and easily achieved, he gets to cross a small item off a list. Then he has the feeling, "I solved that problem." Success. This sense of "mission accomplished" causes a release of dopamine: he feels good about himself; he feels that he can trust himself. It also causes a spike in serotonin, which is a pleasurable brain chemical giving him the feeling that he has the right to relax. Every time he reaches a small milestone in this way and checks a box, not only does he experience pleasurable brain chemistry, but it also creates the perfect environment to replenish testosterone. Only if he has fully exhausted his testosterone levels will his body be able to rebuild testosterone through relaxation. He needs the frequent experiences of pushing through challenging obstacles, being successful, feeling good about himself, and thus earning the right to relax and rest. This creates a positive loop, causing a man to feel better and better about himself and to be more and more confident in his ability to create results.

Just for the record, it is not the same for a woman. She can achieve a lot in her day, but she will not get the same sense of accomplishment and release because she does not run on testosterone in the same way. Women do make and keep promises, but generally, they do so to deepen and improve their relationships with other people. This is why women experience much higher levels of stress in work environments that were designed by men. The entire environment has been created to accommodate a man's way of pushing through and then relaxing.

By making short-term doable promises and sticking to them, a man experiences greatness and strength. It activates the part of the brain that is called the "reticular activating system" that keeps him focused on what he needs to do to achieve his goals. When he makes a solemn promise, "I will do this; I promise to do this," it activates him to follow through as well as to get the support that he needs.

All of these stages are needed for a man to feel good about himself. He has long-term goals and visions. He sets very short-term milestones that he can achieve, hopefully on the same day that he set them. By achieving these short-term goals, one by one, he then feels he has earned the right to relax and rest so he can get ready to achieve the next milestone.

This is why when a man retires, he often goes into a decline. Insurance companies tell us that the risk of death or heart attack goes up dramatically after a man retires. His testosterone levels drop because he no longer has a commitment to taking action every day. The whole cycle breaks down, and he goes into a decline.

Promise When Your Heart Is Open

You make the best promises and commitments when your heart is open and your sense of vision is strong. This is why, in every culture, the lifelong commitment to marriage is initiated with a wedding. The environment is made extraordinarily beautiful, everybody wears their very best clothes — often bought newly for the occasion — and there is abundant beautiful music and food. Everything is instilling a sense of pleasure into your heart. Then, with everyone closest to you witnessing the words, you make a solemn promise to your partner to stay present through thick and thin. Now, every time you feel tempted to break your promise but you keep your commitment to loving deeply, it realigns you to the openness and clarity you had on the day of the wedding.

Arjuna says: John and I created the material for this book during many meetings at his house. We recorded everything, and it was transcribed. Then I had an open window to work on the book and to put it all into one final version. The problem was that this window occurred while I was in one of the most beautiful places in the world, in Greece. Every morning, I had a huge challenge: wake up, stretch, and face an almost impossible choice. There were dozens of voices in my head. Athletic Adam wanted to run on the beach. Lazy Larry wanted to stay in bed. Friendly Phil wanted to seek out fun people to have coffee with. Exploring Eric wanted to hop on the scooter and tour the island. There were not many votes for sitting down at a computer, indoors, to work on another chapter when there were so many alluring distractions outside. But I had had such a good time working with John on this book that every time I thought about keeping my commitment to finishing the book, it bound me back to the sense of vision and clarity we had shared in creating the material.

Sometimes you will feel stressed, out of balance, angry, afraid, or numb. Then your heart is no longer open. That is not the time to make fresh decisions or to change your promises. At the times when you are no longer in touch with your promise, you lose energy and aliveness. Then, simply by keeping your word and by acting as if you still want to do the thing you promised to do, it brings you back to balance. It connects you back to the time when your heart was open and you made the commitment. So keeping a promise is a conscious practice of coming back to the time when your heart was most open and your head was most clear.

Not all of us are going to stay aligned with our mission and purpose all the time. When you keep your word, you find that depression or lack of energy or entropy and lethargy dissipate very quickly. It does not require you to change your mood or to be perfect; it only requires action. That becomes a tool for realigning yourself for who you are at your best.

When you are aligned with your soul's purpose, that is the time to make commitments, and that is also the only time to change commitments. Never change a promise when you are out of balance.

Do It Anyway

When a man feels stressed, he may want to forget or change his commitment because he forgets his sense of purpose, and he just says, "I know I said I'd do it today, but I'll do it next week instead." When he does that, his personal power decreases, he loses trust in himself, and his problems gets worse and worse. The same does not apply to women. We have noticed that when women are stressed, they hold on more tightly to their commitments and feel burdened. By holding on more tightly to what she said she would do, she denies her fluctuating feelings, which makes her more stressed.

If you want to build muscle, you need to lift weights at a gym on a regular basis. When you increase the weights, you do not say, "This feels uncomfortable. I don't feel like doing it today." You made a commitment, and you do it. That is what strengthens physical muscles. Strengthening your personal power as a man is just the same: by making doable promises and then getting them done. One of the symptoms of having the personal power to get things done is a sense of confidence, a sense of clarity, and massive amounts of energy to follow through. When you see someone doing something with great confidence, it was because they spent years practicing and overcoming their resistance, staying to their schedule, keeping their word, and creating results. We may think, *One day I will have the confidence, and then I will take action.* But it works the other way. You do what you said you would do, step by step, and it builds confidence.

This does not happen by having things come easily but from all those times of difficulty when you go back and practice and take action. You do not have to be perfect at something to build confidence; you simply have to overcome your resistance, again and again, to doing what you said you would do. That is how we strengthen and grow our masculinity.

Most of the men we interviewed for this book spoke to us about a sense of calling. It may have come in isolation on a retreat, it may have come in prayer, and it may have come with a teacher or a mentor. It is the moment where you feel called by a force that your mind cannot understand but that is palpable. Some people might call that God or spirit or even your deeper true nature. When you serve something bigger than your mind, which you cannot rationalize, then keeping your word means to keep realigning to that sense of calling. At this point, the masculine part of you is responsible for doing what you said you would do, but the feminine part of you becomes receptive to the whispered command of that force beyond your own understanding.

WHAT GETS IN THE WAY?

Here are some of the parts of every man to be mindful of that can get in the way of the hero's journey to learning to trust yourself more in keeping your word.

Rigid Rodney

If you were raised in a way that you were told to keep your word always, no matter what, you may have developed habits of rigidity where following through without sensitivity to the environment can make you less trustworthy instead of more. You might have been shamed, humiliated, criticized, or even physically punished for not following through. A man who has been put through harsh overtraining in this way keeps his word out of fear of punishment rather than integrity. Then he stays the course no matter what, even when it is no longer serving anyone. A good antidote to this kind of conditioning is to regularly review your commitments and to make sure that they are still in everyone's best interest and then, if necessary, to revise them.

Flowing Philip

Some men either live in reaction to that kind of very disciplined conditioning, or they were never held accountable to follow through on anything. Either way, too much attention to what feels good in this moment will not only cause other people to trust your word less, but it will also diminish your trust in yourself. When a man sees himself as untrustworthy and weak and lacks confidence on following through with things, it erodes his feeling of worthiness and of being whole and complete.

This is very much like eating ice cream or cake, which initially tastes good. If you keep eating sugary things day after day, you will not feel good in the long run. On the other hand, if you make a sacrifice, abstain from ice cream, and choose instead to eat vegetables and salad and nourishing food, it may not give you so much immediate pleasure, but after a week or two, you will feel much healthier. That is very similar to how you make decisions to keep your word each day. If you make decisions based on immediate pleasure or avoiding discomfort, it is like the initial rush of ice cream. But there is not much sustained benefit in this. When you do things because you said you would do them, it may feel uncomfortable or seem like a sacrifice in the short term, but it will lead to a much greater sense of sustained wellbeing in the long term.

Over-Promising Oliver

It is important to find a level of commitment to goals that you can realistically achieve within the time you set. Trying to make a commitment to change everything all at once can weaken you rather than help you grow. In this way, New Year's resolutions often cause a man to trust himself less because most people do not follow through with them. It is better to make small doable commitments each day and then to keep them, no matter what. People who have trouble paying their bills often tend to talk about "financial independence" and making millions of dollars through ambitious schemes. People who pay their bills on time usually just think about the next step. Start with small manageable goals, keep your word with those, and you overcome your resistance to following through that increases your personal power and confidence.

Stressed-Out Steve

When you feel overwhelmed, upset, overtired, or angry, these are the times that you are most likely to want to break your commitments and change the plan. But that is the worst time to make decisions. If you make decisions at this time, they are likely to be least aligned with your long-term vision, and following them will lead to a spiral of feeling weak, not following through, and therefore feeling weaker. And down it goes. When you feel emotionally imbalanced, it is better to make no decisions, but instead do a rigorous workout, or meditate, or just wait until you have had a good night's sleep.

Excuses Eduardo

Sometimes it will happen that you break your word. We are all human despite our best intentions. If you break your word, there is no need to offer a long explanation of why. It really does not help anybody. If you are late, and you were caught in a terrible traffic jam, and your phone had run out of juice, and... and... and, the only important information needed is that you were late. Offering an elaborate story for why you did not do what you said you would do identifies you as a victim of circumstance. You have to hypnotize yourself with your own stories before you can sell them to other people. So you convince yourself that you live a life out of your own control.

We have both noticed that women hate men for giving excuses. Men often assume that if they offer a good enough reason, that should be fine for her. She is much more interested that you understand the effect that it had on her, that you recognize the impact of your actions, and that you do not consider breaking your word to be normal behavior. Offering an excuse gives a woman the idea that it could easily happen again. When you have broken your word, there is no simple pill and no perfect thing to say. You will need to ride it out. But there are a lot of things that can make it worse, and making excuses is at the very top of the list.

If you break your word, be careful about focusing on the other person's upset feelings. "I'm really sorry I was late; there was a traffic jam, I'm really sorry that now you are emotionally upset and reactive." That is a way of pathologizing the other person. You might as well say, "I'm so sorry that you overreacted. I'm so sorry that you are neurotic and insecure." Later we will suggest some better things to say.

Unfocused Frederick

Often, we feel like our attention is being pulled in so many directions at the same time that it can feel like it is being pulled apart. That is why it is important to choose the time of the day when you feel most quiet, focused, and clear and write your list of commitments in that state. Then just keep to it, and slowly cross items off one by one, throughout the day. If you notice yourself losing focus, it is a good idea to have some tricks up your sleeve to clear your head again. Exercising, drinking water, getting fresh air, or scanning the body will all help you return to the state where you know what to do.

THE PRACTICES

Set Reasonable Goals at the Start of Every Day

Once a week, or even once a month, you may want to look at the bigger picture: the overall direction that you choose to focus your energy on. These may be bigger and broader goals like getting closer to your partner, being a good father, completing a website, or finishing a project in the house. But these broader goals do not belong on your daily list. Each day, make a list of five and ten items that you can easily accomplish that day. If you have a job where you are told what to do, and these five to ten items are not work related, they may just be just five minutes each. It is important, in order to develop the habit of trusting yourself, that you do set small tasks each day and check them off.

There are many excellent task-management systems that you can use to do this. The one that we like the best is called Asana. It is available on the Web, but also as an app for your phone. You can toss ideas and projects into it as much as you like. But then you can organize them into different categories. "Upcoming" would be the tasks that are current, things that you want to get done in the near future. "Later" is a place where you can store tasks that you are not working on now. They get hidden until you are ready to move them into "Upcoming." "Today" is limited to the things that you want to do before you go to sleep. Be very mindful of what you put into the "Today" category because you need to learn to trust yourself to truly cross everything off before you go to sleep.

Once you adopt a task-management system like this, it is a good idea to give a trusted friend access. This could be a professional coach, or a colleague, or it could just be a buddy. You can support each other to learn to be accountable.

Do the Hardest Thing First

Once you have your tasks for the day, evaluate which one you are most likely to postpone. This is very likely to be the task that has the most long-term benefit for your life but does not seem to be urgent. Brian Tracy has written one of the best books we know about this topic: it is appropriately titled *Eat That Frog*. You may remember the story of Huckleberry Finn, who said that if you eat a live frog first thing in the morning, you can be confident that you will not have anything else as difficult to do all day. Have the same attitude about keeping your word. Make sure that every day there is there is at least one thing on your list that is visionary, inspiring, and that is a bold step towards your greatness. Do that task first. If necessary, get up half an hour earlier than you need to, and reserve it for that most important step.

Arjuna says: This is how I worked on this book. Every day, I would wake up and go through my morning ritual of stretching, meditation, and putting something in my belly. And then, before any email or phone call or any other task, I put in at least one hour on this book. If you have a creative project like this, make sure that it is always the first thing you do.

Celebrate Your Victories

Every time you complete any task, however small, give yourself a reward. If you have ten tasks on your list for today, and the shortest one is only five minutes long (for example, sending an email), the reward could be quite short and sweet. Stand up and stretch, go outside and breathe some fresh air, or eat a small snack that tastes delicious. When you complete bigger tasks, particularly when you "eat that frog" first thing in the morning, it is very important to fully enjoy that feeling of "I did it... I'm amazing... I'm a rock star." Then it is time to reward yourself with the gift of whatever you most enjoy. This might be making love with your partner, going out to a café or restaurant for something delicious to eat, or even treating yourself to a massage.

Many men overlook this phase of celebration and indulging yourself. To some, it does not seem "manly." But once you understand the brain chemistry involved, you recognize that giving yourself rewards is also a discipline. It is the time when your brain can release dopamine and serotonin and testosterone levels will be replenished. Unless you reward yourself, you will not have quite the same stamina to jump over an even higher hurdle next time.

Modify Your Commitments

Technology is changing so fast that different cultures are influencing each other very quickly. And our global financial structure is so unstable that you cannot run on a predetermined strategy anymore. So we emphasize being a lifelong learner rather than somebody who is knowledgeable. This requires flexibility and the intelligence and sensitivity to change your strategy and your goals as circumstances change. At least once a week, review your long-term objectives and overall direction. If possible, do this with a coach or someone you trust. It is important to do this when you are feeling balanced, calm, full of energy, and connected with your mission and purpose. Learning how to accept defeat early in the process, and how to abandon directions that are no longer fruitful, may be more important to your confidence and success as a man in the world than pushing through no matter what.

What to Do When You Break Your Word

Everybody sometimes gets caught in traffic, misses a deadline, or commits to too many things within an unrealistic time period. You will almost certainly break your word from time to time, and then you will likely disappoint people and diminish your trust in yourself. There are ways to navigate these difficult times that will minimize the damage, however, and also leave you feeling good about yourself.

Here are some tips on how to be with somebody else when you have broken your word:

Tell me about how this has impacted you...

How can I make it up to you?

I am fully responsible, and I do not want this to happen again.

John says: I was teaching a seminar in San Francisco. I get very inspired and carried away when I am teaching, and I forget about time and also about the rest of the world. So the seminar ran late, and I forgot to call Bonnie to tell her where I was. When I got home, she was angry and hurt. I listened to how this had impacted her (she had cooked a nice dinner for me) and how she was feeling emotionally. I made sure she understood that I was hearing her. I said to her, "I am sorry. I was inconsiderate and insensitive." She nodded her head. Then I said, "Next time I'm going to ask my organizer to keep an eye on the time. If we are running late, I'm going to ask that person to call you. I do go to a timeless place, and I realize now that it's unrealistic for me to be responsible for this alone." Bonnie relaxed and smiled back at me. She was happy in a way that she would never have been if I had spun her a hard-luck story.

Forgive Yourself

When you break your word and do not complete something that you committed to, it is not only the other people in your life who you need to clear it with. It is also important to restore your trust in yourself. Once a man gets used to himself as being untrustworthy or "flaky," he loses his self-confidence, his testosterone levels drop, and his relationships suffer. So, if at the end of the day there was something important that needed to be done and you did not do it, sit down—for real—and say to yourself this:

> *I have good intentions.*
> *I have vision, and I want the best for everybody.*
> *I forgive myself for not completing this.*
> *I wipe the slate clean, and tomorrow is a new day.*

For those who choose to run fast in life, they will inevitably sometimes fall down. If you have decided to make a difference to the world through your life, as John and I both have, you will inevitably have triumphs and defeats. When you fail, it is time to pick yourself up and move ahead. You have the right to fall down when you are a man on fire with inspired certainty.

FOR WOMEN

The great majority of women we have both worked with say they want to be with a man they can trust. For a man to do what he said he would do, but also to tell the truth about it, is one of the most critical factors for a woman to be able to relax and open her heart. Of course, intelligently choosing a man who has a basic level of integrity is important, but there are also things that you can do, as a woman, to bring this out in him.

Make It Safe for Him to Tell the Truth

John says: I have a coaching client who lives with his girlfriend. He also has an ex-wife with whom he had children. Sometimes he wants to spend time with his ex-wife and his children, but then he always lies to his partner and says "I'm meeting with some of the guys from work." He told me that he lies to his partner because if he says, "I'm going to meet my ex-wife and my daughter at a restaurant tonight because we like to go out sometimes and have a family reunion," she becomes extremely jealous, upset, and angry. Therefore, he feels that he cannot tell her the truth.

Men do not feel good about themselves when they lie to you or withhold information. They do so when they feel afraid of the consequence of telling you the truth. A man is sometimes afraid of a woman's reaction. When a woman becomes emotionally dramatic, a man makes a note to lie to her next time. The key is to tell him how you feel and expose your vulnerability. This brings you closer, and he will feel more inclined to be open and honest with you as well.

Call Forth His Deeper Integrity

There are times when you may even serve him by getting a little fierce. Arjuna says: I remember many years ago, at the beginning of our marriage, I was completing my book *The Translucent Revolution*. It was an unrealistically ambitious project involving 170 interviews and massive amounts of research. It took the best part of several years of my life to complete. One morning, Chameli and I were enjoying the morning together. Then I said to her, "I have to go now. I have to work on my book." I could see a flicker of admiration in her eyes. Her knight was going to slay his dragon now. On the way down the corridor, from our bedroom to my office, I noticed that the door to the linen cupboard was ajar. When I tried to push it shut, the door was sticking on the hardwood floor. Without hesitating, I went to the garage and grabbed a couple of saw horses and an electric saw. I took the door off its hinges to cut a quarter of an inch off the bottom. As the noise of the saw reached the bedroom, Chameli came out. The adoring look was gone from her eyes; now they were glaring. "What are you doing?" she asked me. I proudly announced I was trimming the door: "For us... baby." Like a real hero. "Are you crazy?" She barked at me. "Stop wasting your precious time. Go to the office and give the gift you were born to give."

Not every woman is prepared to communicate in this way. And certainly not every man is ready to hear it. But I must tell you, in thirteen years of marriage, this moment was one when I felt most loved, most seen, and most supported. She showed me in that moment that she saw me deeply, including my deepest potential and my habit to get distracted, and that she would not settle for anything less than the best in her man. Experiment with your man by calling forth his deepest gift, and see how it goes.

Ask Clearly

When you can see that he is distracted and off track, he is probably already feeling down. This is not the time to tell him that he is a failure or a wimp or disgusting to you. Instead, you can help a man to increase testosterone and to feel good about himself again by making requests of him with things he can do for you. If there is something he can do that you would appreciate, tell him clearly.

"There is a pile of boxes in the garage, which is getting in the way when I go to the car. Would you break them down for me?" A man who is feeling unmotivated, who has lost his mojo, will often be delighted to be given a simple task that he is able to complete and that will give you happiness.

When a woman can make requests of a man for actions he is able to complete, it not only increases the love between them, but it also motivates him to get back on track with the rest of his life.

Do Not Blame Yourself

If you suspect that your man is lying to you or withholding important information from you or even if you think that he is cheating on you, please honor your feelings. As a woman, the blood flow to the parts of your brain responsible for feelings, and therefore for intuition, is much greater than for us men. Maybe it is a cliché, but most people agree that women are more intuitive. It can drive you crazy if you suspect something and then get the message that you are overreacting and being neurotic.

Arjuna says: I was approached recently by a man who wanted me to coach him and his wife. He told me (confidentially) that he had been having an affair for several years but now had broken it off. He said that his wife suspected something but could not prove it. He wanted me to coach them with the objective of calming her down so she could become "less dramatic." Unfortunately, this is not the first time I have heard a man make a request like this. He was lying and cheating on her, but he saw the problem as being all with her overemotional reactivity. I told him that I could help them but not in the way that he was suggesting. Instead, I coached him in learning practices to be truthful and facing the consequences. I supported her to tell the truth about what she was feeling, in her body and in her emotions. It was a wild ride for a while. It only took about a month, and the whole drama had passed. Once he started to be truthful with her, she relaxed and eventually forgave him. The more relaxed she became, the more truthful he became. Now they are back in a harmonious marriage.

As a woman, please honor your feelings of intuition. When something feels "off" in some way, you are not going to feel happy by being rationalized out of it. Trust what you feel, be honest about these feelings, and then find a way for your man to be truthful with you in a way that does not create drama.

A CONSCIOUS MAN:

MEET IVAN MISNER, FOUNDER & CHIEF VISIONARY OFFICER OF BNI

Keeping your word as a man is extremely important. It is about your integrity, a word that comes from the Latin, meaning to be complete or whole. I think it is important to understand that integrity is a standard you apply to yourself, not a sword that you wield against others.

My family always had dinner together around six. We would ask each other, "What did you learn today? What's something interesting today? What did you enjoy?" When my daughter Cassie was eight years old, she did an arts and crafts project in school where they made little pipe-cleaner men. At dinner that night, Cassie gave me her pipe cleaner-man, whom she had named Bob, and told me she had made him for me. Kids give you stuff all the time, but I wanted to acknowledge her and express that I really appreciated it. So as an off-handed comment I said, "I will take Bob with me everywhere." She seemed moved by that, so I had to make sure to keep my word.

I travelled a lot back then, and still do. I'm on the road twenty-six weeks a year, sometimes more. I take Bob with me all around the world. I'm not even sure if she knows I always have Bob with me, but he is always in my briefcase. One day she had a ceremony, and I felt really bad I couldn't be there. So I got a camera and took picture of Bob and me in the mirror. I said, "Bob and I wish you the best of luck in your ceremony." She loved that e-mail. She loved it so much that I began asking people to take a picture of Bob and I where I went. I'd say to a stranger, "Hey would you take picture of me and Bob, right here next to Eiffel tower?" And then I would send the photo to Cassie.

One time I asked Penny Power to take my picture in Kuala Lumpur next to the Twin Towers. I took Bob out and she said, "What's that?" I said, "It's Bob." "Why are you holding a pipe-cleaner man?" she asked. So I told her the whole story. She took my picture and then asked if she could take a picture with her own camera, too. No one had ever asked to do that before, but I agreed. The next day in her speech, Penny talked about people staying connected to one another and the importance of maintaining that personal connection. Then a photo came up on the screen of Bob and me. "Here is one of the ways that Ivan stays connected to his family," Penny said, and then she told everyone Bob's story.

What started as me giving my word to my daughter became a movement, however small. Bob is now on my Facebook page. Whenever I go somewhere, somebody always asks me, "Do you have Bob with you?" I've kept my word to Cassie for decades now. And she knows whenever I travel because everywhere I go, people take pictures of Bob and me and post them on my Facebook page.

Sometimes keeping your word seems like the simplest thing. But it can end up being one of the most important things in your life. Years ago I made a simple comment: "I will take Bob everywhere with me." But this seemingly simple comment created an incredible connection between my daughter and I. It's really important to understand that even simple promises can be meaningful to your relationships many years later.

Chapter Nine

HIS HUMOR OPENS HEARTS

When writing this book, we initiated several polls asking women what qualities they most looked for most in a Conscious Man. The most common answer was, "He makes me laugh." It is not necessarily that he cracks jokes, or that he is funny, but simply that "He makes me laugh." Out of interest, we have also asked men what qualities they find most attractive in women. It is very rare for a man to say that he wants to be with a woman who makes him laugh.

It is considered to be a very geeky and not a cool thing to do: to try and analyze humor. In a display of outrageous bravado, we are going to attempt to do this now, but do not try it at home; it can be dangerous.

A Conscious Man knows how to bring humor into a situation from his inner disposition more than any particular action or words. He has just enough distance from his personality and the dramas of life that he can laugh at himself. He takes things less personally, and instead of getting upset, he has a sense of lightness. But you cannot fake that by reading a set of instructions. It comes from genuinely seeing beyond the drama and having a sense of play.

You can make people laugh when you have just the right balance of involvement and detachment. You are involved enough that you can empathize, listen, and feel. But you have enough distance to be able to see the humorous side as well. With too much involvement, you overemphasize and become emotionally dramatic. And with too much detachment, you become remote and distant. When these two exist together, it creates laughter in the people around you.

Of course, there are many kinds of humor. Sometimes humor is a way of masking pain, and then it become cynical or even cruel. That does not really open hearts. It simply lightens a burden for a few minutes. The kind of humor that is a gift to other people, and makes a Conscious Man attractive, often begins with his ability to laugh at himself. All of the men we talked to for this book had their own version of this, and our favorite was this story from our mutual friend, Ivan Misner:

> When my first book came out, I had the opportunity to do
> my first live TV interview in Connecticut. My publicist told
> me it had to be visual. I had no idea how to make business
> networking appear visual, so I had to put on my thinking
> cap. I am an amateur magician, a member of the Academy
> of Magical Arts in LA. The keyword here is "amateur." So
> I asked my publicist, "What if I do a little magic trick on
> the TV? The host could hold up the book, and when she
> opens it, I could grab it away from her and say, "Careful,
> that's hot!" Then flames would come out, and..." She agreed
> to my plan.

I went to the studio, and I was waiting in the green room with my magic trick ready. There were many other guests there. I was really, really nervous. Then I saw a man walking down the corridor dressed as an American Indian, another dressed as a sailor, then a police officer. We heard over the monitors the host announcing: "Tonight we have the Village People... and also Dr. Ivan Misner talking about business networking..."

Really? I thought to myself. I go on after the Village People? So I added a little more of the flammable powder for my trick. This was going to have to be really good. Then the Village People went live on the show. The audience went crazy. I was thinking now that I would be a complete embarrassment. So I added a little more of that flammable powder. And what was the last song that the Village People did? YMCA. Talk about visual... the entire audience was on their feet. Now I knew that this would be the most embarrassing day of my life. I added a little bit more of the powder. Then the director came into the green room. "Who's Dr. Misner? We need you real quick." They told me I had three minutes before going live. A man was putting a microphone behind my jacket. I was trying to explain to the host about the trick, so she would not be shocked. "When we get to the end of the interview, would you mind holding my book, and when you open it, I will say, "Careful that's hot..." But then the director interrupted, and said that he didn't want the book in the shot, that there would be an image of the book on the screen, and he walked off. The host could see that I was upset, and said, "Look, I'm the host; what do you want to do?"

I told her: "Hold up the book and at the very end, I'm going to say…" But now the microphone was on, and director could hear us conspiring, so again he walked straight up and said, "I don't want you holding up the book. Now you're on in 4 3 2 1…."

The host whispered to me, "I will do it anyway. I'll hold up the book and you do whatever you want to do."

So we did the whole segment, and it went well. When we got to the end, she held up my book. "I have a copy of Dr. Misner's book here," she said.

"Careful!" I said, on cue.

"Why?" she asked.

"Because it's hot!" I said. I had put about ten times more of the flammable powder in the book than was advisable. There was a huge flash. She screamed and jumped into the lap of her co-host. I stomped on the flaming book with my foot. I didn't realize that a flash like that blinds all the cameramen. So they were all standing away from their cameras, rubbing their eyes.

The host was still sitting in her co-host's lap: "Thank goodness I didn't swear on live TV," she said.

"New pants for her please," said her co-host.

My publicist looked at me, and said, "That was definitely visual. But I think we should leave now."

So in most states in America I am considered a business networker.

In Connecticut I am considered an arsonist.

We have heard Ivan tell this story several times. Audiences love him for it because he has made himself the fall guy for his own humor. But what is always most enjoyable is to watch the expressions on his wife Beth's face. He wins her heart every time he tells the story. She adores him for it.

In relationship with a woman, this style of self-effacing humor can break the tension of dominating or being dominated. It lightens the mood. Many men feel caught between either doing everything she wants and trying to please her or digging his heels in, which creates tension. Humor breaks that tension. A man who gives too much or tries to please a woman in every way, loses her respect. He becomes a puppy dog. Instead, he can respond to her demands with self-depreciating humor, and it gives her a greater gift than obedience; it gives her the gift of lightness.

Humor at Home

A woman appreciates when you are sensitive to her needs and feelings, but when you become overly sensitive to your own, it reduces the polarity of attraction. The middle ground between emotional indulgence and cutting off is to bring her a sense of lightness and humor. It reminds her that life is a game. To enjoy playing, you need a mixture of connection and lightness: of holding on and letting go together. These are the two forces of love. Relationship works well when a woman is holding on a little more. She is more involved in the drama and the feelings. The man brings the lightness: with his palms open. Oxytocin is the attachment hormone. Testosterone is the letting go part. This is the dance. First she holds on, and he lets go. He gives her the gift of more lightness so she can find herself again. She lets go, and he moves in a little closer. This dance of more connection and holding on, balanced with more detachment and letting go, is made delightful through humor.

Humor is how he breaks the cycle of stress. Change is always somewhat stressful. Under moderate degrees of stress, a woman becomes more emotional, while a man becomes more detached. Adrenalin in a man causes testosterone levels to go up, which lessens his ability to feel emotion. For a woman, she has eight times more blood flow to the hippocampus, the emotional parts of the brain, which means she becomes more emotional under stress.

Under extreme stress, the opposite happens. A man will become emotional when the stress is too great to handle through action or when he gets burned out. A woman closes down under extreme stress and becomes cold and detached.

When you bring humor to her, helping her see the playful nature of things, it dissipates her stress. But you need to be sensitive to when it is time to empathize and when it is time to zoom out. At times of mild stress, when you are feeling more detached and she is feeling more emotional, your humor can help her to reflect on her reactions and release stress through laughter. When the stress has become too great, when you have become emotionally reactive, and she has become cold and cutoff, humor will feel inappropriate to her and will get rejected. That is when you need to be empathetic: caring, connecting with her deeply for her to be able to feel and open her heart again.

Guy Humor

The kind of humor that works well between you and other men is very different from kind of humor that a woman will appreciate. We often say things to other men that could sound offensive, but we both remain spacious enough so that it is humorous. This is a good preparation for being with a woman, so when she gets critical, we are trained to not get offended. But if you say offensive things to a woman in a spirit of "just kidding," it will generally not open her heart at all.

Arjuna says: A few years ago, I was invited to a barbecue party to watch the fireworks on the 4th of July. It was a neighborhood party when many households were gathered together by the side of the lake to share food. When I arrived, one of my best friends was helping himself to the food at the buffet. A woman who I did not know walked up to me to welcome me to the party. Then she proceeded to introduce me to my friend, not aware that we knew each other: "Arjuna, please meet Larry..."

In a manner that was totally familiar to Larry and myself, I reached out to shake hands with him and said, "Wow, you're an ugly bastard, aren't you?" This was normal banter between us–guy talk. But the woman dropped the plate she was holding and screamed. Things that men find funny together are often not remotely funny to women.

For many of us, the practice or training in learning to laugh at ourselves may not come naturally. But the good news is that we are highly trainable as men, and even the most serious, nerdy, and tense guys, like we once were, can learn to open hearts through lightness of being with a little practice.

WHAT GETS IN THE WAY

Here are the parts that we all have, the voices that will get in the way of your humor as a gift.

Ambitious Alfred

When we get obsessed with wanting to win the game, rather than playing the game, life becomes about wanting to prove ourselves, and we lose the perspective of play. A man who talks a lot about his own achievements and accomplishments will rarely be able to open hearts through humor. Then he protects himself and defends his valuable reputation, and the playful aspect is gone. He makes himself available as a target for other men's humor rather than a source of humor himself. It is the mixture of having a strong sense of mission, together with the ability to take space and create distance, that allows him to be playful about himself.

Self-Righteous Robert

As men, we all carry the momentum of wanting to be right about everything. This is the legacy of the family patriarch: he cannot be questioned on his opinions and his ultimate authority on all subjects. When we get attached to wanting to have the last word in an argument or to be right about the facts, our capacity to open hearts through humor will then go out the window. But at the same time, in the midst of a heated argument, the gift of humor can be the most powerful gift that a Conscious Man can bring to dissipate tension.

Over-Empathetic Emanuel

A man who has learned to feel too deeply and to empathize with other people will become a great listener, a great shoulder to cry on, but too much empathy blocks his capacity to give the gift of humor. Many men over-empathize as a reaction to, and a compensation for, the old macho stereotypes of our fathers and ancestors who were dogmatic and authoritarian. When you become overly identified as a kind man who holds hands with another, listens deeply, gazes meaningfully into someone's eyes, and never judges or pressurizes, you may also become the kind of man who is an expert at supporting another person to stay trapped in their drama. When empathy is balanced with detachment and the capacity to see everything with a touch of lightness, it then becomes the gift of humor.

Drama-Queen Desmond

Whenever we have not taken enough space, particularly over a longer period of time, we enter into a phase of burnout, and absolutely the first symptom of that is that we lose our perspective and sense of humor. As we mentioned above, when a man is under mild stress, he becomes more action oriented and less emotional. And when his stress level goes beyond a certain point, he becomes more emotional. It is impossible for a man give the gift of humor when he has let his reserves drop below a healthy level.

Enlightened Eric

Probably the kind of men who have the greatest difficulty in taking themselves lightly are those men who have identified themselves as being "spiritual." When we emphasize spaciousness, detachment, and meditation too much, we also lose playfulness. To be able to play requires involvement and detachment at the same time. If we only have the detachment, with no involvement, we quickly become too serious and boring.

THE PRACTICES

Shared Challenges with Your Friends

Arjuna says: In the Awakening Coaching Training, we recommend a simple and fun way to get started on taking yourself less seriously as a man. Get together with a few of your friends and a video camera, and set each other small challenges that you can only accomplish when you have some degree of detachment. You can set the bar as low or as high as you like here. Go together into a city, where there are plenty of people. Then give each man a small challenge to perform, which just takes a few minutes. For example, he could go to a place where music is playing and dance wildly. He could even invite a stranger to dance with him. Or he could approach an old couple, arms and eyes wide open, calling out, "Mama? Papa?" Once you get into the spirit of this, there is an infinite variety of fun practices you can come up with together to help each other take yourselves less seriously. It is a great idea to record these practices on a video camera or smart phone. Later, you can share them on social media to break the habit of seriousness with a wider circle of friends as well.

I had a coaching client, years ago, who was a professor at a large university. He was one of the top authorities in his field in the country. He had grown up the youngest of eleven children and was always being teased. So he studied hard and became a professor: a very serious man. He got trapped in this identity. He remained a very serious guy with his wife and his children and with everybody. His life was completely dry. He came to me for coaching. We worked with this using a tool called Radical Releasing, but finally it was time for a practice run to see how non-serious he had really become. He was going to give a lecture in a big auditorium at the university. I suggested to him, before he went to give the lecture, to go to a costume store and buy a tail, like for a cat, that he could attach to the back of his pants.

He walked into the lecture hall and began to give his lecture, facing the students in the normal way. But then, at some point he needed to turn around to write something on the whiteboard behind him. The students started to laugh. They pulled out their cell phones to take a picture of his tail. His practice was not to say anything, or react in any way, but just to carry on giving his lecture. That one incident completely broke his identity of being the serious and tense professor at the university.

Your Most Embarrassing Moment

Just like Ivan did earlier in this chapter, think about the most embarrassing moments of your life, and practice making them into great stories. When you can make yourself the butt of your own joke, that is the best way to open hearts and to give the gift of humor. A self-depreciating story, well told, will cause people to laugh at you, and laugh with you, and love you, all at the same time.

Taking on Roles

A great way to open up more humor in your relationship, or with your family, is to be willing to identify the parts of you that get most serious and contracted and to turn them into Walt Disney cartoon characters. Do this for no longer than five minutes a day. It is like homeopathic medicine: less quantity can create a more powerful effect. For example, you might recognize that you get serious and contracted whenever practical tasks need to be accomplished around the house. You want things done your way. In a moment like this, you could remember to become "The Commandant" for five minutes. Speak with a thick German accent. Stare at people in an intimidating way. Bark orders. If you exaggerate enough, it becomes a source of delight, a walking, talking, art-form instead of something serious. If you tend to get contracted and over identified with being emotional, you can exaggerate this and become the drama queen for five minutes. And if you get serious and contracted when you feel jealous, you could become Luigi, the jealous lover from Sicily. If you can play with your most serious and contracted parts of yourself for a few minutes a day, with the collaboration of your family, it is one of the best ways to open up humor.

Standup Comedians

If you feel that you would like to open up the current of humor more in your life as a man, a great way to get that flowing is to watch standup comedy. Humor with heart has a certain flavor to it. You cannot exactly learn to be funny from a step-by-step instructional manual, but you can acquire humor by being influenced by other funny people. The Internet is packed full of the best standup comedy, often in small, bite-size chunks. Watch the late and great heart master Robin Williams or Jerry Seinfeld or Russell Brand or Eddie Izzard. Each time you watch a clip, take a pause afterwards to notice how you feel. Did it open your heart and make you feel lighter? Or was it cruel humor? If it was a live performance, look at the reactions of the women in the audience. Some jokes cause people to laugh but with a mild look of disgust and embarrassment at the same time. Other jokes bring laughter but with tears of feeling touched at the same time. When you watch great comedians, take a pause to feel what made you laugh. This practice will naturally overflow into opening more hearts yourself with your own humor.

FOR WOMEN

When a man takes a step with the intention of lightening your heart through humor, he is taking a bigger risk than you might realize. For most men, it is an act of courage and vulnerability to aim to be funny. He is walking on the edge. He may successfully open your heart and touch you and lighten your day, which is what he wants. But he may equally get it wrong and become irritating and annoying. Then he feels a sense of failure.

When your man has the generosity to step out on a limb and aim to bring humor to you, do your best to let yourself be lightened. If you want a man who is going to make you laugh, you have to be willing to laugh as much as possible when he is funny. If you kill his humor, as some women do, or ridicule it, do not complain that you have a guy who does not make you laugh any more. You have got to let yourself be lightened when he tries to lighten you. That is a mistake that some women make when they are down in the dumps and their man does something a little crazy or out of the box. She is stubborn and holds onto her mood, and then he is not going to take that risk again.

It can be vulnerable for a man to be humorous. If you want him to be funny, tell him when he is funny. Just as it is great for a man to tell a woman repeatedly, "You look beautiful," for he can say that to you many times a day and it is not too much, so you can tell a man that he is funny as often as you want to, and he will like it. Tell him "You are a funny guy... you crack me up..." He hears these as encouraging words.

There is nothing worse for a man than humor falling flat and leading into an empty silence. When he aims to make you laugh, it is one of the ways he tries to give you a gift. You can get more caught in feeling and drama than we do, and so it is something we can offer you to lift you out of the story and to see the absurdity.

There is so much that you give to men. You remind us to feel, to pay attention to what is here in this moment, to smell flowers more, to notice colors more. Meanwhile, we can help you to expand beyond the immediate feeling of emergency.

A Conscious Man has to constantly monitor the situation to be sensitive to when his humor is going to lighten you and when is it going to be an irritant. For example, if you are upset because you might miss the ferry, he might say, "Don't worry; I've got this. If we miss the ferry, I have a plan B. I have an inflatable dinghy in the trunk of the car." That might lighten your mood and help you to laugh at your own concerns and worries. But when you are upset because someone has just died, that is not a good time to be humorous. A man has to constantly monitor when his humor is going to lighten you and when it could feel insensitive.

If his attempts at humor feel inappropriate, please find a way to tell him without shutting down his intention to give you something. When it feels off, you could say, "This is not the right time now to make jokes. You are a funny guy, I love it when you make me laugh, and I am sure I will laugh later. But right now, I just need you to be here with me."

There are kinds of humor men share together as men that can seem cruel and hurtful to you: "You are an ugly bastard... just kidding." That kind of humor does not generally work for you, but we don't always remember that. There is a kind of humor that is cruel and hurtful that can mask something else. There is a kind of humor that lightens you, when we are laughing at ourselves, and it helps us for you to point this out in an encouraging way. Laugh fully when it is funny. That gives you the freedom to point out when our humor is unkind. A Conscious Man is very trainable to learn the difference between these two.

A CONSCIOUS MAN:

PAUL SCHEELE, FOUNDER OF LEARNING STRATEGIES

O ne of the key things about turning a situation around for the better is the ability to reframe it as a bright spot in the grand scheme of things and then highlight and emphasize that.

I remember a very dark time for my wife and me. Our middle son, John, was eighteen, and had developed a marijuana habit without our knowledge. He had also been breaking into garages and finding things that he could sell at pawn shops, and he'd even stolen some guns from his friend's father. This was enough to set off some pretty serious alarms. The S.W.A.T. team was called to see if John had the guns hidden on him. They didn't want to take any chances.

Because we knew the judge in our county who had signed the warrant, he said, "Paul and Libby are a great family. There has got to be something going on, so please knock, don't just bust down the door." When the S.W.A.T. team came and knocked on the door, Libby offered them coffee. That's just the way we are. I was in England at the time doing some training, and didn't know anything about what was unfolding at home. They apprehended my son, and although there were no guns in his possession at the time, they hauled him off.

He was placed in the county detention center for a couple of days. When I arrived back home, I found out the only way he could get out was to go directly into a drug treatment program. We managed to scramble around and find one, which was not easy to do on short notice. The twenty-one day inpatient treatment program was about a hundred miles away from our house, and we were able to bring him to the treatment facility and get him checked in.

Two nights later we went and met with one of the counselors at the facility to learn a little more about the program. At some point in the conversation, she looked at Libby and me and said, "I want you two to go into Al-Anon." We didn't understand. "What for?" we asked.

"You need to work on your codependency," she said.

Libby turned to me and said, "Codependency? I'm not codependent, am I?" Of course that cracked me up. It's the perfect question for a codependent to ask. "Am I?" I had heard the joke years before, that when a codependent has a near-death experience, someone else's life passes before their eyes.

Immediately upon hearing that question and seeing the humor in it, I said, "Great question, Libby. Would it be okay with you if I'm not codependent anymore?" At that point she got it, and she started laughing. Since that day, it's been one of our favorite lines.

It turned out to be a wonderful situation for our son. He was released within eleven days. He's a great kid—he kept his job and kept going to the community college. There was a stay of adjudication for his problems and his court records were expunged He maintained his relationship with his girlfriend, who he eventually married, and we now have a grandson.

To this day when John writes me a Father's Day card, he always says, "Thank you for loving me while I had to do what I needed to do to find myself." Even in the darkest times Libby and I could see that we had an opportunity to take care of ourselves and be a loving presence. When someone has a chemical dependency problem, you have to remember that you didn't cause it, you can't control it, and you can't cure it. The only thing you really can do is take care of yourself and your own peace.

Chapter Ten

HIS SEX IS A GIFT OF LOVE

Men today face challenges with their sexuality that our ancestors did not face. For the most part, in previous generations a man paid very little attention to a woman's needs. He worked hard, he built-up stress and tension in his body, and then, as long as he had done his duty and provided security for the family, he saw it as his right to have sex with his wife. For the most part, she regarded it as her duty and even an obligation to fulfill his needs. We know that today this sounds preposterous and absurd. Simply dip into the greater part of our literature from before the 1950s, and you will discover that it is true. When William Masters and Virginia Johnson conducted research at Washington University in St. Louis on human sexuality, and for the first time documented the phases of a woman's orgasm, it was regarded as obscene and unscientific by their colleagues. We have come a long way.

Although we have made huge advances in just two generations in understanding sexuality, and respecting both a man and a woman's needs and pleasure, these advances have also made sexuality much more complex and challenging for a man than it used to be. To recognize this challenge, we need to understand the biology.

When a man is attracted to a woman, particularly one who he does not yet know well, dopamine is released in his brain, which is a precursor to the production of testosterone. It gives him pleasurable feelings, it motivates him to take action, and it gives him focus and interest. One of the many functions of testosterone is faster reaction times: the feeling of needing to take action immediately. In an emergency, this causes more glucose to go to the muscles so he can run faster. But it also regulates a man when having an erection. So when a man is turned on, the hormones create the sense of "I want to have that. I want to get closer to, and even inside of, what I'm attracted to." The testosterone does not only cause him to experience pleasure, but it also causes him to be ambitious for more. He wants to go from first base, to second base, to third-base, and then for a home run. He wants more and more and more: that is the nature of desire. Then, at the moment of orgasm, everything changes. Prolactin is released, which inhibits desire, and he wants to pull away and go to sleep. A release of serotonin in the brain causes him to feel euphoric. Since a man is often laying down in a bed when he has sex, and often the room is darker, serotonin converts into melatonin, and he wants to go to sleep. All of the above process used to happen quite automatically and unconsciously for a man before the "sexual revolution." Because dopamine is released so much more with someone new, men would often get married, create offspring with their wives, and then have affairs with other women. It was the newness that created the right brain chemicals to start the cycle again.

Today, in addition to the possibility of having an affair, a man's challenge with his sexuality is further complicated by the enormous availability of sex over the Internet. When a man watches a woman, or even a couple, having sex on a screen and he masturbates, he will release huge amounts of dopamine, much more than he would with regular sex. During this kind of impersonal sex, very different brain chemistry is being produced than during a real intimate encounter. It becomes like a drug where a man then wants a more and more intense, novel, unusual experience to keep driving the dopamine levels up. Watching porn, from a biochemical perspective, is extremely similar to taking cocaine.

When a man has sex with a woman he loves, the biochemistry is quite different. It can be a much richer experience but in a very different way. This is his challenge. Because the elements of novelty and risk are gone, his brain produces less dopamine, and hence he has less lust. When a man has sex with his intimate partner, it often begins with talking together and flirting. Both partners may be feeling stressed from the day, and she will lower her stress levels with the production of oxytocin. To be ready for sex, she needs some time to talk and share and flirt. They then may move together into a phase of soft touching and caressing. This will increase oxytocin levels for both the woman and the man. This brings his testosterone levels down, and he may no longer feel drawn to having sex. Then he thinks to himself, I wanted to have sex. Why is this happening to me? One solution to this problem has been the massive commercial success of Viagra and other similar drugs. It fools the body into creating an erection without the usual brain chemistry being involved.

Focus on Her Pleasure

But there is also another solution, which works better in the long run for everybody. Conscious sexuality for a man means recognizing that sex is a shared experience. It is pleasurable for him but in a much deeper way when it is pleasurable for her as well. Remember from previous chapters: when a man feels he has an important job to do, a mission to fulfill, especially one that is a little challenging or that requires endurance and stamina, it will boost his testosterone. Giving a woman pleasure, and ultimately giving her deeper and more fulfilling orgasms, is not only a win for her (in obvious ways) but is also a win for him. This sense of making a difference, of serving something beyond his own needs, now balances the increased oxytocin created through intimacy with the testosterone created from having an important job to do.

There is a phenomenon in psychology called the conditioned response. If a man does something but feels unsuccessful after it, the next time he does it he will have a drop in testosterone. If you walk into a room and people stand up and clap, then just walking into the room the next time will cause an automatic surge in testosterone. If you walk into a room and people boo or ignore you, then testosterone will drop the next time. It is just the same with sex. It is a conditioned response. If you have sex with your partner, and she is not completely satisfied, over and over and over, it will cause testosterone levels to go down. In this case, because it affects your erection, it becomes a downward spiral where the lack of confidence negatively effects sexual response, which then further lowers confidence. Eventually, you say to yourself, "Why should I even bother?" Then jerking off to porn on the Internet or having an affair with another new stranger seems more interesting and less complex. On the other hand, when a man recognizes the cycle, and focuses primarily on her needs and deep satisfaction, it spirals the other way. When she has a deep satisfying full body orgasm, some part of him feels confident: "I did that... I'm the guy..." It means that the next time they have sex, he will feel more confident, more testosterone, and a stronger erection, which will often contribute to more satisfying sex, greater confidence, and on and up we go. Yeehaw!

This does not mean that it is necessary to give a woman an orgasm every time you have sex. That could become obsessive. It means that he is primarily attentive to her needs, to her biology, and to knowing that she is generally deeply satisfied in her sexuality.

Conscious Sex

In order for a man to shift his attention in sex from primarily focusing on his own pleasure to focusing on hers, he needs to slow down. And that, of course, in today's society, is a challenge on its own. For this reason, there has been a surge of interest in the last decades in practices from Oriental cultures like Tantra, Taoist sexuality, and related books have been jumping off the shelves at bookstores. The essence of all these teachings is how to breathe, slow down, and to allow sex to last longer.

Couples who start to explore sexuality in this kind of conscious way soon discover that both men and women bring habits dating back hundreds of years that need to be recognized and overcome. For men, patriarchal religious traditions have conditioned him to be ashamed of his sexuality but also convinced him that women do not experience sexual pleasure. Frequently, such traditions have encouraged a kind of misogyny, where a woman is seen as one who sucks his energy and makes him weak. Hence many traditions have emphasized celibacy as a way for a man to reach his highest potential. Or, rather than learning to be a good lover, puritanical religious traditions just advocated avoiding sex altogether, except for when making more babies within marriage.

Our collective past has also caused woman to contribute towards this kind of unsatisfying sexuality. Historically, sex was the only way that a woman could feel she had power over a man. In every other way he was dominant. So she would bring him to ejaculation quickly, partly to get it over with, and partly because it was her way to get her own back and to sap his power. Now, as both men and women are discovering a more conscious sexuality, we are all learning to recognize these inherited habits and to move beyond them.

Making Love to Life

This kind of more sustained sexuality, which recognizes the needs and pleasure of both partners, can also become a kind of "dress rehearsal" for the way that you "make love" to the whole world in the rest of your life. For a man, when he focuses on bringing her to the peaks of pleasure, he feels good about himself. He knows that he has the capacity to penetrate her with his steady masculine presence, and then she opens to him, she gives love to him, and becomes more beautiful in his eyes. After they have made love, when he goes out into his daily life, he carries with him this same sense of confidence. Now he feels instinctively that he can penetrate his world with his masculine presence, and he can open opportunities and hearts. He knows that people will love him for this, and then the whole world also becomes more beautiful in his eyes. In this way, making love becomes something like a spiritual practice, similar to meditation, yoga, or prayer. It prepares you to bring forth the very best of yourself in every aspect of how you live.

A woman experiences the same thing in her own way. When she receives him through her vagina, the more aroused she becomes, the more her heart opens. She pours love into him through her breasts and her heart.

Then, when the lovemaking is finished, she has more love, more creativity, more compassion, and more wisdom to share with everyone in her life.

Many couples today are also learning how to circulate energy during sex, which also prolongs sexual arousal, and builds this experience of giving to each other. For a man, learning how to spread arousal from the genitals into other parts of the body particularly means moving it up the spine so that the sense of being invigorated, refreshed, and energized by sex becomes stronger.

Conscious sexuality means to make love with your whole brain awake. The reptilian brain — connected to our basic animal instincts — is activated and responsible for the most basic thrusting energy that makes sex exciting, passionate, and satisfying. The middle brain — responsible for feeling — creates intimacy, connection, and the subjective experience of love and bonding. The prefrontal cortex being awake and active also allows you to make conscious choices about circulating energy, breathing mindfully, and prolonging the sexual experience by being aware of what is happening for both of you. A couple that is exploring in this way can then enjoy all kinds of sex: the animalistic wild ride, a quickie to regenerate yourself, and the slow home-cooked sexuality which requires a whole evening to be set aside.

WHAT GETS IN THE WAY

Porno Pete

When a man watches porn, his brain is getting the message that dozens of scantily dressed women want to have sex with him. They have taken their clothes off, which usually means only one thing to him. So it gives him the illusion that he has somehow succeeded with his flirtation and seduction and won them all over. But he never actually went through that process.

His testosterone levels spike in an unrealistic way without having been built slowly, which causes him to disconnect from his emotions. Without the intimacy of touch, dopamine is not balanced by estrogen, and the body chemistry gets thrown off. It makes it more and more difficult to then have satisfying sex with a real partner. By continuously stimulating high levels of dopamine, receptor sites down regulate and become less sensitive. As a result, when he goes back to his wife, it is more difficult to find her attractive. Pornography, like heroin, over stimulates dopamine in the brain so that normal stimulation is no longer as exciting. Porn is training a man's body to have sudden peaks of dopamine and testosterone, without the regulation of oxytocin, and the more he does this, the more he brings the same chemistry into the bedroom. Now, the oxytocin produced through intimacy is not met by the sustained gradual release of testosterone, and he becomes less sexually confident. What is he to do? He gives up quickly and goes back to masturbating in front of the computer. He gets addicted to new and unfamiliar women with no personal contact or touch at all. Research shows that both with prostitutes and models on the Internet, men very rarely go back to the same woman again. He is training his brain towards arousal in the presence of novelty with no intimacy.

The solution is to find ways to restore newness and excitement to real live and intimate sex with someone you love. This will restore the balance of dopamine, testosterone, oxytocin and prolactin and cause sex to become exciting and pleasurable again for both partners.

Promiscuous Paul

Changes in society all over the world have made it much easier to have multiple sex partners. This is not the same as it used to be when a man would have a secret affair or go to a prostitute and keep it all hush-hush. Today, if you choose to, you can be quite open and relaxed about being sexually active as a single man. Equally, even if you are in a relationship, some couples are exploring "polyamory," which means to have ongoing sustained sexual relationships with more than one person at the same time. While it is a wonderful thing to have so many more choices than were available in the past, it is also equally important for us to be aware of the consequence of those choices. When you hook up with someone new, and particularly if you have sex on the first meeting before you have gotten to know each other, it is going to involve a very different brain chemistry than in intimate sexuality. Similar to with porn, having sex on a first date will cause a spike in dopamine and testosterone, which is not balanced by oxytocin. This kind of lifestyle can easily become addictive to a man where he feels increasingly more compelled to have sex with every attractive woman he sees. The actor Russell Brand did us all a huge service by being honest about this kind of sexual addiction and how he recovered from it. A lifestyle of easy casual sex will shift the brain chemistry in a way that makes it more difficult and more challenging to have an ongoing and possibly more fulfilling relationship with one person.

Sedentary Steve

If you are at the office, dealing with emergencies and deadlines, you will be stimulating the fight-or-flight part of the brain. If all of this is happening while sitting in a leather chair, your body will get the signals of emergency without using up the stress hormones through activity. In the same way, watching a football game or an action movie creates chemicals of excitement and emergency, but these get trapped in the body because there is no physical activity involved. Today's lifestyles frequently cause us to stimulate the hormones that are precursors to action without actually taking the action itself.

A sedentary lifestyle prevents us from being fully in our bodies. Breathing becomes shallower, and we accumulate more adrenalin and cortisol that never gets balanced or released. All of this interferes with the normal biochemistry of sexuality. The best way to address all of this is regular physical exercise and deep full body breathing, and exercising and building your muscles by going to a gym two or three times a week.

Workout Walter

Notice, we said two or three times a week, not two hours a day, every day. Building muscle mass too much in relation to actual physical work can reduce testosterone and impair sexual desire. Testosterone is stored in the muscles. If your storage capacity is much greater than the actual testosterone you are creating, you will have less testosterone being released into the blood. It is like having massive 6-inch-diameter water pipes in your house but an insufficient supply of water to flow through them. The result will be weak water pressure. Research done with professional bodybuilders has shown that their testosterone levels are below average. The body uses the testosterone to rebuild the muscles, and then there is nothing left over for libido. Back in the 1990s, before the Internet, there were many muscle magazines full of pictures of men in their 20s and 30s. These magazines were also full of advertisements for libido enhancing products. Now why would men in their 20s or 30s need libido enhancing products? It is because excessive working out reduces testosterone to abnormally low levels and kills your sex drive. The only solution was to have sex with women a man did not know, where the newness and challenge and danger would artificially peak testosterone production.

Premature Peter

The length of time it takes for a man to ejaculate is determined by methylation: the utilization of sulfur and vitamins in the body. Men with slow methylation ejaculate more quickly, and vice versa. Slow methylation is primarily determined by genetics but exacerbated by diet, health issues, and stress. Luckily, all of this can be overridden by epigenetics. In a way, conscious masculinity is all about epigenetics: allowing conscious choices and understanding to override automation and instinct. A man who ejaculates more quickly than he would like to, or more quickly than allows his partner full satisfaction, can easily learn how to sustain his erection for longer periods through specific practices. We will describe these in the next section. The important thing is not to get fixated on lasting forever, or never ejaculating, or always ejaculating every time, but to be sensitive and conscious of what works best for both you and your partner.

THE PRACTICES

Structured Sex

If you are in a relationship, one of the best ways to bring your sexuality back into a healthy balance that is optimal for you and your partner is to have a structured sex date once a week. For the other days of the week, you can do whatever you want, whenever you want, in whatever positions you want. But once a week, following a simple protocol will keep you in a balance that feels good to both of you.

It is a great idea to set this up as a date in your calendar in advance: "Tuesday night, 8pm, is our sex date. It does not matter what else comes up; this is a commitment that we keep." Arjuna says: One woman I was coaching felt very committed to this idea but had difficulty in engaging her husband. So she said to him, "Every Tuesday at 6 PM, I will be getting sexually aroused in our bed for an hour. If you'd like to join me, you are always welcome." It did not take him long to get with the program.

John says: I have guided many couples in a practice I call "Polarity Sex." It has three stages.

Stage I: She Gives Pleasure to Him for Five Minutes.

While making out, kissing, and touching, her focus is on getting him aroused and giving him pleasure through his whole body but including touching his penis and possibly oral sex as well. The idea is simply that he gets aroused but without ejaculation.

Stage II: He Brings Her to Orgasm.

The man turns his attention to completely focusing on her pleasure. He can begin by touching and stroking her body, which will increase oxytocin and lower her stress. Once she feels more open to him, he can massage her breasts for several minutes and then move down to her vagina. The man slowly brings her to orgasm with his tongue, or his finger. This stage could involve intercourse as well, so long as he is absolutely confident that he will be able to bring her to orgasm without ejaculating. This stage will take as long as she needs and may require patience on the man's part. He should be very attentive to her feedback, both verbal as well as sounds and body movements. He brings her to orgasm through a combination that she most enjoys of clitoral stimulation, stimulation of the G spot, and deeper penetration.

Stage III: Shared Lovemaking

After she has climaxed, he enters her and they make love together. When a woman climaxes, her vagina will bulb and then contract. This is the physical symptom that she has reached a point of satisfaction. Anything after this is deepening her more into that pleasure. Now when he enters her it will be a tighter fit, they will both experience maximum stimulation, and it will be a much deeper way of making love.

He will feel less of an urge to ejaculate after she is already feeling satisfied. The lovemaking will be naturally slower with both partners breathing more deeply, and there is a much greater possibility of building energy together and entering plateaus of sustained pleasure and intimacy.

You can find out much more about polarity sex in the book Mars and Venus in the Bedroom.

Conscious Cultivation

If you are a single man, the easiest way to prepare yourself for conscious sexuality is to bring yourself to a state of mild arousal and then to breathe and deliberately circulate that aroused energy down into your perineum and then up your spine and the rest of your body. This is a practice men have been doing in China for thousands of years known as the "Big Draw." It is considered to be one of the most essential keys to longevity, good health, and satisfying a woman. It is relatively easy to learn and has powerful results within a few weeks.

Cultivate Choice about Ejaculation.

Whether you are single or in a relationship, the key to practicing conscious sexuality is to be able to separate arousal from ejaculation. This is at the essence of every tradition which has emphasized sexual cultivation. You can practice the Big Draw even if you are in a relationship, so you bring more conscious choice about if—and when—you ejaculate when you make love. You can ask your partner to help you become aroused, but then instead of moving directly into penetration, you can ask her to help you spread the energy through the whole body as you breathe deeply. She can stimulate your penis with her hand or mouth. When arousal increases to the point where orgasm will be coming soon, ask her to move the stimulation away from your penis to other parts of the body by stroking and touching the thighs, belly, and upper torso. Breathe deeply together as the energy spreads throughout other parts of the body for a whole body experience. For more information about the Big Draw, or sexual cultivation alone or with a partner, we recommend that you read *The Multi Orgasmic Man* and *The Multi Orgasmic Couple,* both by Mantak Chia.

Another approach to delaying ejaculation is to use a spray that contains lidocaine and prilocaine about fifteen minutes before having sex. Studies show that the use of such sprays causes a man to last an average of 2.4 times longer from entry to ejaculation. Some condoms also have a mild anesthetic on the inside, which has the same effect. The use of sprays or condoms in this way will make it easier to gradually develop other practices of cultivation.

The important thing about any kind of sexual cultivation like this is simply to restore greater choice. It does not mean that it is never good to ejaculate, but it is good to be able to choose how long you last before you ejaculate if you choose to. Ninety percent of this is intention and decision. As soon as you set the intention to be able to have more control over your energy, the practices themselves are very simple and easy to learn. If you do decide to practice more conscious sex in this way, we would recommend that you mix it up with some quickies now and then as well as some wild-go-crazy sex.

Be in Your Body

It is very important in today's fast world to take the time each day to either build muscle or to exercise rigorously. Fully inhabiting your body produces pheromones that are necessary at the biological level to turning a woman on. Physically use your body to the point of exhaustion every day. You can do that with running, biking, the gym, or swimming… The easiest way is interval training. Google it.

If you are going for a walk, run for a minute full out. Then stop. You will notice that you are panting; this is very similar to the breathing that happens in sexual arousal. Bend over a little bit, bend your knees, and lower your head. Allow yourself to take a few minutes to recover while breathing through your nose. After resting for two to three minutes, run full out for another minute, and then repeat the whole process again This is a wonderful interval training technique that can be done with any exercise. It will have an immediately beneficial effect on your sexuality.

Communication

If you decide you want to explore conscious sexuality, it is a great idea to make a plan with your partner. You could read together *Mars and Venus in the Bedroom* or *The Multi Orgasmic Couple*. There are many other books also available which will help you together to move from unconscious and purely instinctive sex to a more conscious sexuality that lasts longer and brings deeper fulfillment to both of you.

FOR WOMEN

We have learned that the most important gift a woman can give to a man is to communicate her needs: to find ways to tell him honestly when she wants to have sex, when she wants to be sensuous and cuddle, and when she want to be left alone. Men have a difficult time imagining or guessing what sex is like for a woman, and unless you communicate, he assumes that it is exactly the same as it is for him, which turns out to be far from the truth. To become more conscious sexually, men need a lot of feedback about what is working, what is not, and when it is time to stop or slow down. You can communicate this not only with words but by making sounds of pleasure or by moving his hand somewhere else.

One of the greatest errors that women make today is to assume that when a man wants to have sex, he is only trying to get off or to release pent up tension. A Conscious Man is motivated to love you deeply, through his whole body, and it feels good to him to succeed in taking you to the moon through sex. Rather than offering him a quickie or oral sex, it may be better to be honest when you are not in the mood but instead to make a date, at least once a week, to be intimate together. This does not even have to involve intercourse: it is simply a firm date to be naked together, to breathe and touch and connect. A date like this is guided by your pleasure. Let him know what you like and how quickly or slowly to move to the next step. You might even like to teach him how you would like him to give you orgasms through your clitoris, your G spot, as well as deep in your vagina. To a Conscious Man, this is a gift. It is a much more fulfilling sexual experience than just getting off.

Some women will sometimes fake pleasure or even orgasm, which trains a man to think he is doing a great job as a lover when he is not.

That is not the best way to bring forth consciousness in a man. When resentments build up between a man and a woman, it affects a woman sexually more than it affects a man. He can still have sex even when there is "stuff" in the air. But for a woman, when there are unresolved feelings in the relationship — resentment, distrust, hurt, or distance — it makes it difficult to genuinely open up in sex. Since he does not understand that so well, he may put his partner under pressure and tell her that she is not contributing to the relationship. Many women then just do it anyway, to please him and to do their part. Under these circumstances, a woman wants to get it over with quickly. She will look for the shortest route to get him aroused so he can ejaculate. The key here is to talk about feelings and to encourage him to practice listening.

Both men and women come from thousands of years of woman's sexuality being less important than a man's. For a Conscious Man, the practice is to focus more on your pleasure. It recreates balance and retrains him to be more aware sexually. We might think the opposite is also true, that for a conscious woman, the practice is to focus more on his pleasure. But we have all been doing that already for thousands of years. It will help a man much more to practice focusing on your pleasure. Focus on what feels good to you and what opens you, and find ways to communicate that to him. That will give your man the opportunity to succeed in being a good lover. Remember, in every way men feel better about themselves when they are able to succeed through action.

If you are single, it is equally important to be honest with yourself and everyone else about what you really want and what you do not want. It is important to learn how to say "No" to a man, without the fear of rejecting him and losing him.

Arjuna says: Monika contacted Verena Hirschmann, a certified Awakening Coach in Frankfurt, Germany. She wanted to open to a relationship in a new way than she ever had before, and Verena is a specialist in this field. Monika told her coach that she always ended up with the wrong kind of a guy: married men cheating on their wives, drug addicts, men incapable of making commitments, or those who were abusive. She admitted that she felt aroused and more alive around such men. Verena coached Monika for several months to recognize and dissolve the habits that attracted the wrong kind of a guy.

In the third month, when Monika met Rainer, she was nervous. She knew that she wanted to have sex right away as was her habit. "Find five of your best girlfriends," Verena advised, "who really care about you and want the best for you. Make a clear agreement with them that you will not have sex with Rainer until they all meet him and give the thumbs up. You may not be able to anticipate unhealthy symptoms in a man, but your friends will notice it for you."

Monika was nervous that Rainer would lose interest if she did not have sex with him quickly. So Verena said, "Tell him, 'I really want to have sex with you, I feel attracted to you, and I also want to get to know you better.' If you simply say 'I don't want to have sex with you,' it will turn him off. But if you can say, 'I'd love to have sex with you, but it doesn't work for me to have sex right away. I need to get to know somebody first,' then he will not feel rejected; he will feel inspired. When a man does not get what he wants right away, he has to earn your openness and your trust. That is how he learns how to bond with you. If you make it easy and have sex right away, he never learns to bond, and there is the likelihood he will move on."

Verena's advice to Monika worked out very well indeed, and it broke a lifelong pattern. We have both worked with so many single women who benefit from this kind of support: to express attraction to a new man but at the same time claiming the right to wait for the right time.

A CONSCIOUS MAN:

LEE HOLDEN, CHI KUNG TEACHER

When I was in college, sex and women took up a great deal of my attention. Sexual energy was very interesting to me, but I was not very skillful at it. I didn't know how a woman's body worked; I didn't even know how my own body worked. Things either took too long, or I ejaculated too quickly. Then one day I stumbled into a bookstore and found the spiritual sexuality section. There were books there by Mantak Chia about how you could have multiple orgasms, transform and sublimate sexual energy into consciousness and spirituality, and have a deeper connection with your partner. I was amazed!

After university, when I was about twenty-five years old, I went to Thailand to help Mantak Chia write some of his books. He gave me an old manual and said, "Can you turn this into a book?" The manual was about how ancient Daoist practitioners were helping people to arrange marriages. He wanted me to write it in a more modern way, so that a person could tell if they were sexually compatible with someone. It was later published as *Sexual Reflexology*.

Some of his senior instructors were also there, including a French woman who was about fifteen years older than me and teaching many of the classes. She was very beautiful and sophisticated, with a radiant glow. She moved so gracefully, was very wise, and knew all about internal energy arts. I had a puppy dog crush on her, but I never thought I could be her lover because she was way out of my league.._She's going to teach the Chi Kung class tomorrow morning,_ I thought. _Maybe I'll just say something to her._

After class we started talking. I asked her some questions about the book I was working on, and I asked her to tell me about the cultivation of feminine energy. We agreed to continue our conversation over dinner, and we really connected in the restaurant—that magnetic locking-in happened. I could feel the energy elevate. Then she asked me, "Hey, do you want to practice?" I did not know what she meant. She laughed. "I'm not coming on to you!" she said. "Do you want to practice Chi Kung? I can show you how to move the energy in your body, in the way you are asking about for your book."

So we practiced Chi Kung together. We raised the energy, and then she showed me how to create an energetic connection with another person without even touching. She explained to me how people jump into physical sexuality too quickly, when what we are really seeking is the energetic connection behind the sex.

Probably two or three weeks passed without any physical contact at all, just this very intense daily practice. Finally, we did become lovers. It was completely electric, and all the pathways opened quite naturally, which felt like an initiation for me. I learned that if you develop a strong, energetic connection with someone but don't get intimate, the sexual energy rises up from the sexual center and expands into the heart. If you have sex too quickly, this energy can drain away quickly. It won't make its way throughout the body, and it especially won't get to the heart.

Ever since that meeting, sex has never been the same for me. It is so much more than just a physical expression. It's emotional and spiritual; it's also in the heart. Everything blends together into one energetic soup.

Conscious sex is an incredible practice: with a partner you can skillfully elevate each other's energy into a very high level of bliss and connection. This is so fascinating to me that I have continued to practice and study with other Daoist teachers to learn more. It has become a rich catalyst for a lot of other work that I do in health, healing, wellness and spirituality.

Chapter Eleven

HE RESPECTS THE GIFTS OF THE FEMININE

As a man becomes more confident and comfortable in his masculinity—settled in his mission and purpose, regularly taking space and reconnecting with his depth, and secure in his capacity to love—he naturally develops a respect and appreciation for the gifts of the feminine because they no longer threaten him. He can recognize the gifts of the feminine without having to minimize the gifts of the masculine.

It is through being receptive, appreciative, and responsive to this feminine energy that a man reconnects with meaning, purpose, and passion. When he becomes too obsessed with action and reaching goals, he shuts off his more feeling side. Then he wakes up every day with another long list of things to do and a knot in his stomach, but no reason to do them. It is by reconnecting with feeling, which means appreciating the feminine, that he rekindles his sense of passion and excitement.

As we will discover later in this chapter, he comes to appreciate the feminine first through the women he is close to: his mother, partner, and co-workers. But this appreciation then also awakens the same feminine qualities within himself. Finally, he comes to recognize this same feminine principle not just in human beings but in all of life. When he walks in nature and sees the dew dripping from the leaves, or hears powerful and emotional music (even if it was written by a man), he recognizes that this is the same universal feminine energy that expresses itself in life everywhere.

So what are some of the qualities that a man comes to recognize and love as the universal feminine? It is a vast and multidimensional subject, so let us just skim the highlights here.

Relational

The feminine in all of us is more receptive and responsive to the needs of others. This kind of natural empathy is the result of being more connected to emotions. Thus, to the degree that you can experience your own feelings, you can also experience other's feelings as well. Masculine power emphasizes the ability to get things done: to set goals and to achieve them, often alone. Feminine power, which often goes unrecognized, emphasizes collaboration, delegation with respect, and empowering others to get things done. A mature and Conscious Man, who aspires to be a great leader, recognizes the need for a balance of these two factors: the ability to take bold action and the ability to work harmoniously with others.

Enjoying the Ride

When a man develops respect for the feminine and moves beyond his endless striving to accomplish, he realizes that his masculine world is black and white. The feminine opens so many more facets to everything so that he discovers life is a multicolored, multidimensional movie.

John says: If I go for a walk with Bonnie, I am thinking of how quickly I can reach the goal. She is walking with me and seeing little flowers; she looks into the distance and sees a tree and the sun setting. She shows me the things I would normally miss. By loving her and deeply respecting her, I have learned to enjoy the ride as well. By hearing her needs and respecting her way, I have become less goal driven. I am much happier and yet I still achieve my goals.

Arjuna says: I remember when we went to buy a vacuum cleaner together at Costco. I went straight to the information desk, not wasting any time, to ask where the vacuum cleaners are displayed. I marched over, did a quick cost comparison — price versus features — selected the right model, went directly to the checkout with the smallest line, and I was back at the car in thirteen minutes. Mission accomplished. Efficient shopping. A few days later, we went shopping again for something that Chameli needed. Almost as soon as we had entered the store, she noticed other things. She saw a scarf that she liked, then she saw some shoes, and then she went to the area where they have millions of different kinds of smells in tiny bottles that you can spray on little pieces of paper. We stayed there for two hours. Finally, we went back to the car. She had one little silk flower, in a bag, with some colored tissue around it. That was all she bought — seven bucks.

"Well," I said, "that was a waste of time."

"What do you mean?" she said. "That was the best shopping day ever." Over the years we have been together she has taught me in so many ways to appreciate the journey as much as the destination.

The Value of Family and Relationship

John says: Before I was married to Bonnie, I was first focused on spiritual goals and then on how I could prove myself in the world. She gave me the awareness that yes, that is important, but time with children is also important, and time with each other is important. By listening to her feelings and recognizing what she needs to be happy, what she needs to receive from me, and what she could give to me, she helped me to regulate my drive.

She has always been really good at communicating that to me in a way I can hear. Now I realize, when I look back over these last thirty years, that I have so many beautiful memories of being with my children — family moments — because my wife taught me that. If I had followed the example I had from my own parents, I would have been a father who was always out at work and who ignored his family to a large degree. When we got married, Bonnie already had two children from a previous marriage. She told me that she did not want any more. I did. So we had to negotiate. Finally, she agreed to have another child if I would promise to be a "50-50 husband" in raising the children. I needed to be as equally involved with them as she was. This awoke feminine qualities in me. I know that I have become a more whole, loving man, and I've had a much happier life as a result of this.

I was sitting at the airport the other day waiting for my flight. There was a man sitting next to me talking on his cell phone. I couldn't help but overhear him. He was working in a consulting business. He was saying to someone on the phone, "I got this great opportunity. It offers twice the money I'm making right now. It's a lots of travel, on and off planes all the time. I would only see my family on the weekends. Why would I want to do that? I would miss all the moments of the kids growing up. I turned it down."

I felt great respect for that man. I leaned over and said to him, "That was the right decision." This was a man who had found an intelligent balance of his masculine and feminine energy.

The Importance of Nurturing Relationship

Men love to fix things. Women typically nurture things. There is a difference. Sometimes it can happen that this love of rising to the occasion of an emergency can cause a man to want to take things apart just so that he can rebuild them. With a motorcycle engine, that may be interesting, but in relationship, it can be chaotic. As a man learns to listen to the wisdom of the women in his life, and so awakens the feminine in himself, he learns how to avoid creating messes as much as how to fix them.

Ivan Misner tells us that in his career of teaching people to network, women naturally have a different style of networking than men do. A man will give you his résumé and tell you everything he has done, everything he can do, and will do. Women, says Ivan, tend to ask more questions: "Where are you from? What's your family like? Do you know Pete and Carol? I think you'd like them. Where did you get that painting? I love it..." Ivan tells us that, as a result, women create many more sustainable relationships within business, create the quality of inclusiveness and team spirit, and now are primarily teaching men how to improve their networking skills.

Taking Care of Yourself

A man who is completely shut off from his feminine side, and who therefore disrespects the feminine in life, will generally have a tendency to push himself to extremes and to burn out. On the other hand, a man who thinks primarily about his own wellbeing and pleasure becomes weak and unfocused and loses confidence in himself. But a man who has learned to balance his masculine and feminine energy understands that he must take care of his own body and respect its needs to be fully of service to others. He gets enough sleep, he takes the right supplements, and he exercises regularly because he understands that this is the essential foundation for fully living his sense of mission and purpose.

Improving the Environment

One of the results of women coming into workplaces that were traditionally dominated by men over the last decades has been a dramatic improvement in working conditions. If we go back to the 1950s, men might be working in poorly lit conditions with bad air and inhumane hours. It is generally women who come into a workplace and ask: "How can we make this better?" Men have focused more on efficiency: "So long as the tool works, let's not mess with it. Let's see how fast we can get the job done." This has been the attitude of slave nations in the past. It is women who have initiated the movement towards more flexible hours, gyms in the workplace, childcare, and the development of human resources to make sure the people are treated fairly. As men have learned that putting emphasis on these things actually helps them to be more efficient in the long run, they come into greater appreciation for the gifts of the feminine.

Loving the Planet

Finally, it is the integration of feminine energy into international politics that has brought awareness to the importance of caring for the planet. In 2014, Tunisia, in northern Africa, revised their constitution to not only assure equal rights for men and women but also to constitutionally protect the rights of the planet. Our good friend Lynne Twist, who has raised more than $2 billion to alleviate world hunger, founded the Panchamama Alliance to help preserve the natural resources of the rainforest. She spent more than a year in Ecuador helping to revise its constitution to include an article titled "Rights of Nature." It is the first constitution in the world to recognize legally enforceable rights of the planet that can be protected in court. In Ecuador, Mother Earth can have her own attorney present to ensure that she gets a fair deal.

Three Portals to Access the Feminine

There are three ways that a man comes into deeper appreciation of feminine energy: in the women around him, in himself, and in life itself.

Whenever you pay more attention to the women around you, to the ways that they respond to life in ways differently than you do, you come into deeper appreciation of feminine qualities generally. It starts with your mother when you were a child and then continues with your sisters, with girlfriends and later with your wife or partner, and also with your female colleagues at work.

The appreciation of feminine qualities for a man is much easier if the women in his life were able to provide him support in his masculinity. If you think about it, it is quite simple. If you have a friend who always sees the best in you, wants you to succeed, and loves you without conditions, you are more likely to respect and appreciate that person as well. If you were loved and appreciated by your mother, and you are loved and appreciated as a man by the women in your life today, you will probably naturally respect and appreciate the feminine. But if your mother was overly nurturing, you may have felt suffocated and then resist and rebel against feminine qualities later in your life. If your mother was overly critical, you may have felt hurt and then resent the feminine. If your mother ignored you or was not there for you, you may have shut down any openness to her and then have become insensitive to the feminine later in life. Fortunately, all of these scenarios, whether seemingly positive or negative, are all automatic and unconscious. With practice, they can all be transformed into a relationship with the feminine that allows you not only to love and to respect women but also to bring forth valuable feminine qualities in yourself as well.

The second way that a man finds feminine energy is in himself. In the past, and still to some degree today, many men have had much greater resistance to accepting their feminine side than women do to accepting their masculine side. If a woman points out more masculine qualities in another woman, it is often seen as an encouragement. "You go, girl! You stand up and show them you are powerful." Women often wear men's clothing and look good. But when a man points out more feminine qualities in another man, it is often heard as an insult. Words like "pussy," "wimp," "girly man," and even "mangina" are used in a derogatory way.

When a man becomes sensitive to his own needs and feelings, or when he allows himself to access the nurturing, care-giving, and loving qualities within himself, he is accessing his feminine side. The iconic psychologist C.G. Jung called this the "anima." He made a really important distinction. If a man completely denies his anima, he becomes hard and obsessively driven, and then he suffers and often causes suffering to others. If the anima becomes more dominant than his masculine side, he becomes feminized, and then he feels weak, uncentered, and lost. He also suffers and withholds his gifts to others. But Jung pointed out that when a man is firmly rooted in his masculine essence, but also connected with his anima as a supportive influence, he becomes a whole and healthy man, who has plenty to give to the world.

Arjuna says: I had a coaching client who was stuck in a corporate sales job. He was continuously faced with deadlines, and he had to make his quota, so he was driven. He made great money, but he told me that his life was flat and empty. So he quit his job. He started to attend Gabrielle Roth's Five Rhythms dance. He grew his hair longer. He took a yoga teacher-training course in Bali. He attended the Burning Man festival. During this year off, he started to notice all kinds of feelings that he had not explored as much before. When he came back into the workplace, he was a more whole man, better able to take care of himself. I have experienced the same thing. For many years, I was a single dad. I had joint custody with my ex-wife, and when the kids were with me, I was the only adult in the house. I was holding them, cuddling them, cooking food, reading stories at night, and playing games. I was a really good father. And it was great for me. It was an evolution. It allowed me to recognize and live certain qualities in myself: now I would call those qualities my feminine side. As a result, my appreciation and honoring of the feminine everywhere has increased.

The third way that a man comes into appreciation for the gifts of the feminine is in the world around him. Now he realizes that feminine energy is not just a quality of women, or even of his own anima, but it exists in all of life independent of human beings.

As we have described in an earlier chapter, when a man gets together regularly with other men, he sees that many qualities he thought were personal are in fact universal to all men: they point to a universal masculinity. In a men's group, you hear other men's experiences, and then you have the reaction, "I have that experience too. That man needs space sometimes. So does he, and him, oh, and him too, and so do I. That man gets driven and fixated on a goal. So does he, and him, and him, and him, and so do I." In this process, as men, we take things less personally. We attribute aspects of being a man not to our childhood conditioning, or even our nationality or social conditioning, but simply to being a man.

The more that we recognize qualities of the universal masculine, the more we can also recognize qualities of universal femininity and love them. For example, you might come home to find that your partner has put three simple flowers in a small vase on the kitchen table. The splash of orange color adds something special to the room. You might think to yourself, *I would never have thought of doing that. It is beautiful. Mary is so good at making things more beautiful.* But then you might reflect that your mother often does the same thing, and so does your sister. Come to think of it, so did your previous girlfriend, and the one before. And, come to think of it, when you meet in your men's group, it's usually — not always — just paper plates and not much decoration. Before too long, you realize that it is not just Mary and your mother and a few other women you admire for these qualities, but it is in most women. It is the feminine. Those same feminine qualities are alive in some men as well. Now you have expanded your appreciation from women to the feminine in a broader way.

Arjuna says: I experience this with Chameli sometimes when we are just fooling around, having fun, laughing, or planning things together. She is being Chameli, a woman from Norway in her 40s who lives in California with her British husband. But then, just in moments, tiny snapshots that open and close again almost instantaneously, I find myself looking not at this woman, but into her. She has become something like a window instead of a woman. And then, in a way that may sound a little too "woo-woo" and

Californian for some, I find that I am no longer relating with a woman as a separate person, but I am looking into something universal, mysterious, and undefined that has the qualities of a universal femininity being lived through one particular human life. When Sherry Anderson became aware of this universal femininity that can be accessed through any woman just like the ocean can be tasted and experienced through any wave, she wrote a book about it and called it *The Feminine Face of God.*

The more stable a man becomes in his own masculine presence, the more he can appreciate and enjoy the qualities of universal femininity — as a constantly changing display of color and energy — and the more he can penetrate it with awareness. When a man steps into life, into the demands and unexpected curveballs of the world, he is now meeting the feminine not just as women but as the display of all life. He brings a conscious, penetrating presence to meet the colorful chaos of the feminine as it displays itself in nature, in his business, in traffic jams, in international politics, and on the Internet. Whenever he meets a swirling, ever-changing, and sometimes overwhelming display of color and sound and sensation and chooses to meet it with courage and generosity, he becomes the universal masculine fully offering its gift to the universal feminine.

The more appreciation he has of the feminine qualities in himself and in women close to him, the more he will love life, and the more he will want to give to life.

WHAT GETS IN THE WAY

Success-Driven Derek

A man has to become aware of his own biology to the degree that it no longer runs him compulsively. The rush he gets from setting ambitious goals and then pushing through to reach them, no matter what, and then basking in a fix of dopamine before he starts it all over again, can cause a man to live addictively. He may spend his whole life desperately climbing a ladder, only to learn too late that it was leaning against the wrong wall. As you appreciate the gifts of the feminine, you recognize the limitations of an exclusively masculine focus. Embracing the feminine brings greater richness to your life. When you make love with a woman, you slow down. You touch her breast, and it is soft. It is not like a man's chest, which you can pound on. To meet with her, everything forces you to soften and slow down. The same is true beyond sex as well. In every area of your life, when you appreciate feminine qualities and also integrate them within yourself, you become a more balanced, mature, kind, and whole man with more to give.

Wounded William

The relationship you had with your mother, as a boy, is absolutely core to your capacity to love and appreciate the qualities of the feminine in your adult life. How did you connect with her? How did she see you? Was she happy? Did you have opportunities to make her even happier? When a young boy grows up with a mother who is basically happy, but then he also has the opportunity to bring her more happiness through small gifts, artwork, and breakfast in bed, he grows up to be a man who naturally anticipates this experience with the feminine. He knows he can make her happier, and as a result feels good about himself. Unfortunately, most of us did not have exactly those circumstances to the degree that we would have liked. We need to heal the past and reinvent a relationship to the feminine that is healthy.

Misogynist Martin

We have certainly come a long way and have more respect for women in society, but the undercurrents of misogyny are still alive and well in the world. Just go to a bar that is mostly populated by men. Hang out for a while and listen to the jokes that guys tell. There still exists a habit of men bonding by speaking of women in a derogatory way. Then it is not just about women; it is a way of denigrating feminine qualities in life but also then denigrating that part of ourselves. Collectively, men still have a tremendous fear of being feminized. It starts with the fear of being bullied at school and then it continues. If a man has become sensitive to his needs, or has feelings, other men may call him a "pussy," or a "mangina."

We have all been raised to experience ourselves and express ourselves in a linear way. If you are a Republican, you are not a Democrat. If you go to five-star restaurants, you do not eat at McDonald's. If you are an atheist, you cannot also enjoy church music. If you enjoy roughing it while camping, you do not enjoy yourself at the Four Seasons. That would be inconsistent. And if you are a strong, dependable, upright, manly kind of a guy, then you are supposedly not also sensitive or influenced by your feelings.

It takes a more mature perspective to realize that you can be this and also have some of that, even though they are often perceived as opposites. Being a Conscious Man means that you can be aware of more things than the linear mind will allow through its filters. You realize that you are multidimensional and you contain opposites. You can have a strong masculine presence; you can powerfully give your gift to the world and be a five-cylinder testosterone machine and still be connected to your feminine energy, feel deeply, and consequently have deep respect for the qualities of the feminine everywhere.

THE PRACTICES

Give Appreciation

As a man, acknowledging and appreciating the feminine qualities you discover in the women close to you, in yourself, and in life around you, will help these qualities grow and magnify. By verbally expressing this appreciation, it makes it even more powerful. Several times a day, make sure that you say to your partner, or to the people you work with, statements like:

> *You look so good today. I love how well you take care of yourself.*
> *Thank you for reminding me to take care of myself too.*
> *The room looks so much more beautiful than I would ever have made it.*
> *It amazes me the way you know how to create harmony between people.*
> *When we go for a walk, you point out all the things I might miss.*

The more you voice appreciation, the more your feelings of respect will grow, and the more you will wake up this valuable part of yourself as well.

Sit and Wait and Marvel

If you are in a relationship with a woman, or even if you work with women, take five minutes sometime to see if you can predict what a woman is going to say or do next. It is a wonderful experience. You might be sitting on the sofa together or sharing a meal in a restaurant. For five minutes, you can continue to be in conversation, but simply allow yourself to get curious. What is she going to say next? Do not initiate any new topics of conversation; leave it up to her. Arjuna says: I practice this often with Chameli. I totally love it. We might be talking in bed together or just sitting on our deck looking at the trees. I go into a passive mode... I just wait. I have realized that I have absolutely no idea what she is going to say next. She is a mystery and a marvel, constantly surprising me. Reminding myself continuously that it is impossible for me to predict her next move dramatically increases my appreciation of her.

Forgive Your Mother

You can do this practice with your eyes closed as a visualization, or you can use a notebook or a journal.

Remember the relationship between your parents when you were a child. Remember the rooms in the house and the views from the window. Now write about this in the present tense from your mother's perspective. As your mother, write about what is frustrating to her. Write about what is disappointing. Write about her concerns. Write about her relationship with your father. As your mother, write about your regrets, what you long for, and what you need. Is she happy? Are her needs met? What makes her happier? What makes her unhappy? What does she love? What is she appreciative of and grateful for?

You are an adult now. You are no longer dependent upon her. As you recognize what she was feeling, as you recognize her frustrations and her limitations, you will naturally grow in the awareness that she gave the best she could within her limited circumstances. This naturally overflows into forgiveness. Out of forgiveness will grow gratitude and appreciation for your mother. She gave you life, she probably cooked for you and nurtured you as you were growing up, and she did her best to support you as you were growing older. The more you forgive and appreciate your mother, the more you will appreciate the feminine everywhere.

If You Had Been Born a Woman

Here is a simple and powerful way to get more connected to your feminine side as a man. Again, you could imagine this with your eyes closed or you could write it out in your journal, but you could equally make this something you share with other men in a men's group—if you have a courageous group of men.

Go back in your imagination to the time when your father made love to your mother so that you were conceived. Imagine the sperm traveling towards the egg. Experience the moment of conception. But now, imagine that this meeting of sperm with egg results in a girl baby instead of a boy. It is still you, but now you are being born into a girl's body. Imagine the moment of your birth, how happy everybody is with this new daughter. What is your name as a girl? Now imagine the room they have given you to sleep in. Notice the toys you play with and the other little girls you become friends with. Move on slowly through your life: the clothes you wear and the games you play as a little girl. Imagine your first day at school and the other girls you make friends with. Continue slowly through your childhood as a girl, and then experience yourself entering puberty. Feel what it is like for your breasts to grow. Experience your first period. Notice how your relationship changes towards boys as you get older. Move through your teenage years, and experience all the things you become interested in and identified with. You can continue to move through all of your life, maybe including getting married and giving birth to children. This is still you but just born into a different body. This is a fantastic practice. You only need to do it once to connect more deeply with your feminine side.

Do Feminine Practices Sometimes

Earlier in the book, we differentiated between practices that bring forth more masculine energy and practices that bring forth more feminine energy.

On the whole, we would say that it is not really good for a man to do feminine practices on a regular basis. But sometimes, give yourself a day where you move completely into feminine practices. Let yourself have time to explore your feminine side. Some things you could experiment with would be these:

Watch emotional movies about relationships, and cry when you feel moved.

Take long bubble baths.

Go shopping for clothes, for several hours, with friends. Try things on, and complement each other on how good you look in different outfits.

Dance in free flow to music.

Go out to a wine bar with men friends. Order white wine or rose and tiny tasty finger snacks. Talk all evening together about feelings and relationships and enjoy gossip.

Enjoy all kinds of sensory experience.

FOR WOMEN

When we speak about appreciation of the feminine in our talks and seminars, so many women tell us that they want to be with a man who feels that way. Women ask us: "How can I bring that forth in a man?" The answer is very simple.

Everything works through magnetism and resonance. It is all done with mirrors. If you want a lot of money, do not spend your time thinking about how poor you are and craving for money. Spend as much of your time as possible feeling affluent and appreciative, and money will flow to you. As a woman, if you want a man in your life who deeply appreciates and adores the feminine, the solution is quite simple. Learn to deeply appreciate and adore the masculine. It will be mirrored back to you. A woman who primarily feels like "I'm a gorgeous woman. Look at me! Adore me!" will attract to herself a man who says, "I'm an awesome man. Look at me! Adore me!"

A woman who deeply appreciates the gifts of the masculine, while remaining confident in her own feminine essence, will attract to herself a man who bows down to her in the same way that she bows down to him. This is not about the adoration of personality but the appreciation of essence. What do you most love about the masculine? What are the qualities that you find in a man that are more difficult to find yourself? Appreciate those, and you will get back his appreciation.

At the same time, make sure that you allow yourself to be adored and adorable. Sometimes a woman needs a little encouragement in allowing herself to dress up in a way that helps a man to deeply appreciate her beauty and to express it. One of the things that men notice and appreciate most about women is when you make yourself look beautiful. This is not just about a man lusting after you. When you wear nice earrings and beautiful colors, paint your nails, or wear makeup that is well done, men love to see it and really appreciate it.

Finally, when he does things for you, make sure that you pause and actually experience any pleasurable feeling that it gives you, and then give it some expression. Sometimes just a little murmur or a smile is enough as the words "thank you" can get so old. Your appreciation for a man's actions will bring forth much more strongly his appreciation of your feminine qualities.

A CONSCIOUS MAN:

ANDREW HARVEY, SPIRITUAL ACTIVIST

The Universal Feminine is the core of my life because what She has revealed to me, in the core of me, is a great, holy passion for the whole of life, for the whole Universe, for all beings, for all created things. The Universal Feminine has revealed to me the glory and the creation of presence in, and as, everything. It has revealed to me the absolute primacy of tender, surrendered, passionate, compassionate love as the key to transformation for both women and men.

I was only twenty-one years old when I was elected as a fellow to All Soul's College in Oxford. But sometimes what you pray for can destroy you. I entered this magical world and wanted to be a part of it, but quickly discovered it was full of egomaniacs and people with terrible despair, doing some really crazy stuff.

Prime ministers visited, along with the Archbishop of Canterbury, CEOs, and ambassadors. At dinner you could be seated next to anybody. This was extremely liberating in one way, and very scary in another. You saw, up close, the people who were ruling the planet. You saw them arrogant, and drunk, and sometimes abusive, fantastically self-pleased. This was a wake up call to me about our culture's condition, along with the condition of masculine power.

I met women there too, like Margaret Thatcher who came to dinner once. A man fainted in front of her. She just stepped over him; she didn't even step down in any way to find out how he was. I saw what happens to the ambitious feminine, too, that allows herself to become corrupted. It was a terrifying education.

I understood from that very early age that the elite that rules us is insane. And that depressed me terribly.

Thank God it did. Because that depression drove me back into the arms of India where I was born. It was then that I really began to embrace the Divine as Mother: the motherhood of God, the embodiment process, this great, holy, birthing process of a new kind of humanity not separated from the creation, not drunk with the creation, but one with the creation.

One day I walked down from the hotel I was staying in to the beach. My mind seemed to crack open, and I saw the diamond-white light of divine consciousness radiating from everything. From horizon to horizon everything was singing. The footprints in the sand were all glowing with light, which revealed to me the sacredness of the whole universe; the absolute presence in and as everything; blessing everything, living in everything, radiating through everything. This astounding, white-diamond light of bliss and love.

That moment changed everything because I realized I knew nothing. I had been trained as an intellectual, as an academic, and here I was having the grace of monumental awakening without any kind of preparation for it. So I knew at that moment that I had to plunge into several mystical disciplines to try and comprehend this experience and experience it from different angles: to deepen it and not to be destroyed by it. The key for me was how to marry the burning passion of the mother with the great peace of the father in the core of myself, so as to birth a new kind of sacred male in myself that is fused with the wisdom, passion, tenderness, and skillful means together with the surrendered feminine. That for me is the goal of my life.

The healing comes from the embrace of the feminine. That is the moment the masculine becomes sacred. Instead of being intoxicated by its own strengths and powers and clarities, it realizes something more beautiful than itself, more beautiful than anything. It pledges itself to serve and honor and salute and protect this in itself and in women and children and animals and the creation. This is when a male becomes a sacred male, a true lover, a warrior midwife of new creation. We are all called, whether gay or straight, to be a sacred lover, warrior, midwife of this creation.

The connecting bridge is love. It is love that congeals the revelations of the laws with the passion to act for justice—and that love is the motherhood of God, that love is the divine feminine.

Chapter Twelve

HE IS AWARE OF OUR HISTORY

In the summer of 2014, in Ferguson, Missouri, an unarmed black man named Michael Brown was shot to death by Darren Wilson, a white policeman. It resulted in some of the most violent riots in modern history. Eric Holder, the U.S. Attorney General, ordered an investigation not only into the incident but also into the entire policy of policing in the St. Louis area. As the investigation got underway, and as reporters swarmed to the area to cover the story, a pattern emerged. People in Ferguson were extremely angry, exasperated, and at a boiling point. They were angry about the shooting of this unarmed man, but that was just the tip of the iceberg. They were even more deeply angry about a long history, which only has to go back less than 200 years to the days of slavery, of black people being mistreated by authoritarian white men. Darren Wilson was acquitted of any crime. But the Ferguson Police Department was placed under investigation by the Department of Justice, which concluded that "the police department routinely violated the constitutional rights of the city's residents by discriminating against African Americans and applying racial stereotypes in a pattern or practice of unlawful conduct." To view this as an isolated incident would be to completely miss the point. If there had never been slavery, if there had never been racism in Missouri, and if in the last few years the Ferguson police force had not engaged in racial profiling, the reaction to this incident would have been completely different.

Arjuna says: A few months ago, I was returning to the U.S. on an airplane from Europe. Sitting in the row behind me was a family from somewhere in the Middle East: a father, a mother, and their daughter. Both the women were wearing hijabs, the headwear common to practicing Muslims. As the flight got closer to San Francisco, the flight attendant came through the cabin asking people to close down their electronic equipment and to put them back in the overhead bin. When she asked this man to put away his computer, he became extraordinarily upset. He started to shout at the flight attendant. He was clearly not just upset about losing a few minutes of computer time. He assumed that he was being racially profiled. I could hear from the assumptions he was making that he must have had years of experience of getting on planes with his Muslim family and being viewed as a security threat simply based on his ethnicity. The request to store his computer did not happen in a vacuum; it was the last straw for him in an endless pattern of feeling humiliated.

Almost every experience we have belongs within a bigger context. When a Protestant from Belfast meets a Catholic from Dublin, they are not starting fresh. Each carries the accumulated experience of many generations back: the hurt, the grieving, the revenge, and the feeling of not being safe. When a Palestinian meets an Israeli, when a black man meets a white man in South Africa, or even when a staunch Republican meets a liberal Democrat, the meeting is never happening in a vacuum. We all carry not only our personal history but also the collective history of many generations to every meeting.

As a man, everything exists in its bigger historical context. Every time you meet a woman, whether your intimate partner or a coworker or just someone in a random encounter on the street, it is not just you—as a man isolated from history—meeting a woman. You are a representative of masculinity, which has its own history dating back thousands of years, and each woman you meet is a representative of femininity in the same way. You cannot escape the reality of this historical context, but consciousness, honesty, vulnerability, and sensitivity transform everything.

So what is our history as men and women? We have talked about this a lot already in this book, so let us just indulge in the briefest summary here. Both men and women have their traditional roles, which existed for countless generations in an almost unaltered manner. Men would go out to work, often involve themselves in danger and accomplishing a mission, and then would come home to rest and recover. Women traditionally stayed home, cared for children, prepared food, and made the environment beautiful. Just within the last two generations, we have seen those traditional roles thrown up in the air. Women began to feel restricted and imprisoned by staying home. They felt stifled in their creativity. They recognized, perhaps for the first time, that they have gifts to contribute professionally just as much as men do. Men equally began to feel imprisoned by a life of rigidity and duty. They grew their hair, rebelled against limitations of time and structure, and learned to flow and be in the moment. But it is possible for reactions to the original stereotyping to equally become another kind of stereotyping, another kind of imprisonment. And now, men and women are rethinking both the traditional roles and their reaction to them and reconsidering what would be a truly liberated choice. We hope that our book has contributed to this last phase for you.

As men, when we introduce this awareness of historical perspective, it includes the awareness of the traditional roles that we lived for thousands of years, the awareness of getting stuck in reacting to those roles, and it can even include the awareness of getting stuck in a reaction to the reaction. Does that sound ridiculously complicated? Let's take an example.

Arjuna says: There is a man I have known for close to twenty years. He is now in his early 60s. His father worked hard his whole life, had very little contact with his children, and died of a heart attack within a year of retiring. My friend became a man who was committed, above all else, to not be like his father. So he grew his hair into a ponytail. He worked part-time because he just could not bear the idea of being trapped in a fixed schedule. He wore loose-flowing clothing, in bright colors. If he made an appointment, he would show up somewhere within three hours of the set time and sometimes not at all.

A few years ago, we had a talk, he and I. Slightly tentatively, and with respect, I asked him if perhaps the intensity of his reaction to making sure he did not become like his father had caused him to conform to another kind of stereotype: the aging baby boomer hippie, complete with the right clothing, vocabulary, and lifestyle. Being an aspiring conscious kind of a guy, he was open to hearing me. He found himself a weekend workshop to do so he could learn new ways to be a man.

Obviously, the person who put that workshop together had yet another formula for how a man should behave. When I next saw my friend, he had started to hold his body rather unnaturally: something like a cross between a sumo wrestler and a sheriff in the Wild West who was about to draw his gun. He began to stare at people when they asked him questions, emitting an unspoken message: "I am a deep man, and right now, I am penetrating you with my awesome masculine presence." He was super serious now and almost grim, a truly superior man. He took up martial arts and talked a lot about "accountability." But he was still late anyway. This new skin of masculinity seemed to me to be just another imitated way of being. It was a reaction to a reaction. Luckily, now that has worn off, and he has developed a sense of humor about himself, so it is a lot more fun to be around him. He had to shift from trying to fix himself and conform to an idea of the way a man should be to becoming conscious of all the different forces that are running his life. Learned behavior creates automation; awareness creates freedom.

As this awareness of our shared history increases, it opens the possibility of taking responsibility for—and even being willing to apologize for—things that you did not personally do. This is a "hot topic," highly controversial, and not to everyone's taste. But it is so powerful when it happens that it is worth a mention.

Arjuna says: Almost 20 years ago now, I was in Sweden leading a five-day retreat for men and women. We were exploring together these kinds of issues of collective pain. The men went off on their own for an entire day and focused on these four questions:

How have I been hurt by women?
How have I hurt women?
What do I love about women? and
What do I want to create with a woman?

Over the course of many hours, we discovered that most of the answers we came up with were collective. One man would say, "I felt hurt when she ridiculed my achievements," and then we would discover that 80% of the men had the same experience. Another man would say, "I felt hurt when she led me on seductively but then pushed me away when I got interested." Again, his experience was not personal as almost every man had experienced the same thing. Then another man would say, "I used a woman for sex, and once I had conquered her, I lost interest in her completely. She went through painful feelings of abandonment." Again, every man could find a memory like that.

In the evening, the men walked back through a snowstorm to the building where the women had been doing the same kind of exercise. Now both men and women had brought to the surface all of their most important memories of being hurt, of causing hurt, of appreciation, and of intention. One by one, a man would stand up, say how he had been hurt in one sentence, and then any woman who could resonate with what he said would stand up and say, "Yes, I did that, and I'm sorry." She might not have known the man personally, but everything that was being said in the room was being spoken from collective masculinity and femininity. After some time, we switched over, and the women did the same thing. One woman after another spoke about how she had been hurt by men, and each time one or more men would stand up, take responsibility, and apologize.

There is of course something completely illogical about a surrogate apology like this. It requires looking beyond your personal actions, and even your personal beliefs and thoughts, to tap into archetypal forces which are collective. This kind of apology is definitely not for everyone.

If you are sensitive and listen carefully, you will continuously hear both men and women reacting to pain from the past. Sometimes it is their own personal past, and other times it is even the collective past of what has happened to men and women in previous generations. If you can find it in yourself to understand when someone is carrying the past in this way to feel regret and empathy and even perhaps to say, "I am sorry you feel this pain," you may become the vehicle for a healing which that person could never get in any other way.

WHAT GETS IN THE WAY

Traditional Trevor

The first layer of automated conditioning that gets in the way of being aware of the habits that we carry over, unquestioned from our parents and grandparents, is our ideas of traditional gender roles. However liberated we may think of ourselves as men, all of us still have knee-jerk habits of putting men and women into pigeonholes. As a man, whenever we assume that a woman cannot do something or understand something because she is "too fuzzy headed," we are falling back into traditional stereotyping. Whenever we make a hiring decision at work or choose a babysitter or a construction worker or a car mechanic or a housecleaner based upon gender, it is a sign that we are running on automatic and still thinking inside the box.

Flowing Philip

We also can get stuck and lose our freedom by getting caught in reactions to traditional stereotypes. We have talked about that a lot already in the book. If you notice yourself unwilling to do something — anything — because you are concerned that it is a traditional macho role, you run the risk of getting trapped into a rebellious reaction. Arjuna says: I was vegetarian for years, in part as a reaction to the idea that real men eat huge hunks of steak. I have also never taken much interest in organized sports because watching football on the TV seemed like a cliché. Then one of my friends, who I greatly admire as a conscious and mature man, invited me to watch the Super Bowl with him and his friends. I went along, not for the game, but because I wanted to spend more time with him. We ate burgers and watched the game. Suddenly, I was hooked, and I realized I had been avoiding watching team sports just because I thought it was part of a traditional masculinity that I was beyond. Let yourself become aware of every habit you have avoided just because it seemed stereotypical, old fashioned, and just like your father. Then ask yourself, "is this really something you don't want to do, or is it just a reaction?" You never know. You might enjoy professional wrestling, the demolition derby, and NASCAR more than you imagine.

No Difference Desmond

When we are in reaction to traditional gender roles, we can also get caught up in the idea that there is no real difference between men and women: in other words masculinity and femininity are just made up concepts. This idea is taught today in many universities: that all gender differences are a social construct. Gender rules are certainly constructs, but there is still our biology, which needs to be honored and respected. We can learn a lot from traditions in ancient cultures in their understanding of gender difference but at the same time maintain freedom of choice. Otherwise, it is a case of throwing the baby out with the bathwater — throwing out the wisdom of the past because we do not want to be imprisoned by it.

The past is past; we did the best that we could do. We were trying to survive. Those were the smartest roles for us to take at that time. Also today, many women still do not feel imprisoned by traditional female roles and do what feels right to them in each phase of their lives. John says: I have the experience of having had a very happy mother who raised her children and stayed at home. She was not tormented that she could not go out and run a business. When her kids grew up, she started her own business. And Bonnie, my wife, stayed at home and raised our three daughters and created a beautiful home and garden. Now they are grown, and she has an active role in our office, but we have always each taken the role in the family that seemed to be the best for everyone at that time.

So long as we feel free to make the best choices today, unencumbered both by stereotyping and reactions to it, we can also enjoy our history and all that it has brought us. You can feel proud of your male ancestors even if they lived within narrower limits of choice than you have today. Most of the cities we live in were built by men. We walk on stairways built by men. We enjoy political freedom that was protected in the past by men. We enjoy medical advances which in the past were mostly pioneered by men. We enjoy majestic art, music, and literature, most of which was — in the past — created by men. None of this could have happened without women. We each played our role. Every single one of our ancestors, with no exception at all, owes his life and everything he created to a woman who bore him in her womb for nine months and then went through an excruciating experience, often risking or even losing her life, to bring him into this world. Our ancestors were raised and nurtured by women, who at that time, if they had abandoned their traditional role, would probably have risked the lives of our forefathers, so that you and I would not be alive today. The traditional roles that previous generations adopted have provided the foundation for all of us to enjoy this moment today.

Projection Percy

We also lose the ability to experience our history consciously by projecting our needs today onto previous generations. For example, if you read novels by Jane Austen or even Mark Twain, you will be introduced to a delightful world gone by where men and women lived within traditional roles but were also happy and experienced love and connection and plenty of opportunities for self-expression. If men or women from today's world were to be transposed now into the 18th century, they might feel extremely restricted. But it is a mistake to assume that we know what people experienced in the past.

When you first have a baby, you might put the baby in a playpen to play. The baby will stay there for hours with a few toys. The baby is not screaming and yelling, "Let me out! I will report you to the authorities!" Later, your child goes to kindergarten and has to remain there under the supervision of an adult until getting picked up by a parent. This does not feel like an imposition to a five-year-old. But try imposing that limitation on a teenager, and you will have a full on rebellion on your hands. To the teenager, you can perhaps say, "You need to be home by 10 p.m." You may get some rolling of the eyes, but you will also probably get compliance. Try imposing that same limitation on your adult child of 25 or 30 years old, and they will think that you have gone completely insane. The limitations that are appropriate at one stage of development will seem unbearable at another.

We frequently make this error of imposing our current stage of development retrospectively on previous generations and then saying, "In the past, women were tortured by men. They were forced to stay at home and not have a career." But is that really true? We do not have any evidence of that from 18th century literature. We might also say, "In the past, men lived imprisoned in a life where they were forced to go to war and work long hours in jobs they hated, and they were not given the opportunity to fully be part of raising children or participating in the household." We have no evidence that Napoleon, Mozart, or Benjamin Franklin suffered in this way.

THE PRACTICES

Ask "Is it true?"

You can learn to become aware of the limitations we impose upon ourselves about what it means to be a man, or to be a woman, by noticing throughout the day when you make an assumption based upon gender. This could be a great practice to bring to your marriage or to your men's group. Just for a few minutes, let yourself speak out loud the assumptions you make about roles. You will probably notice that some of these assumptions are influenced by traditional values, and some of them are influenced by reaction to those values. Here are some examples:

A man should... earn more money than a woman.

Men don't... cook as well as women.

Women can't... understand mechanical things.

Men and women should be equally involved in changing diapers,
dropping the kids off at daycare, and being at teacher's meetings.

None of these ideas are intrinsically right or wrong. The important thing is to question every assumption, now and then, with the question, "Is it true?" This means would absolutely everybody subscribe to this view? If some people would agree, and others would not, then it is not true, per se; it is simply an opinion. Once you recognize that, you and your partner and everybody in your life can choose to create whatever you want together that makes everybody happiest and gives everyone the maximum opportunity for self-expression.

Take an Interest in Your Ancestors

There are some wonderful websites available now that allow you to find out all kinds of interesting things about the people responsible for giving you life. Ancestry.com, for example, allows you to dig back to your great-grandparents and great-great-grandparents and allows you to access documents that give you valuable insight into how they lived. Arjuna says: A few years ago, when I first discovered this site, I spent weeks diving into it. So many other people, who must have been relatives to me in a distant way, had already posted a lot of information. Later, I went with my youngest son to Salt Lake City so he could go skiing there. I dropped him off in the morning at the resort, and then spent the whole day in the Mormon library, where I found birth certificates, death certificates, marriage certificates, military reports, and even personal letters involving my ancestors. They came alive for me. For example, in this way I got to know my great-great-grandmother, Georgia. She got on a boat from Southampton in 1860 to travel to India and marry my great-great-grandfather, whom she had only met once—briefly—at a soirée in London. It was clear from the documents that he traveled to other parts of India frequently on business, leaving her alone with the tea plantation, the servants, and then with young children. I was able to read enough to get a vivid insight into her challenges, the things that made her happy, and finally her death from malaria at 25.

Surrogate Apology

If your partner, or just a woman you know, expresses resentment about the way women have been treated historically, or unfair discrimination in pay between men and women, or violence against women, see if you can find a way to resonate with her experience. You may have voices in your head that want to argue to point out the rough deal that men have had too or to throw your hands up and say, "It has nothing to do with me."

Instead, you might experiment now and then with saying, "Yes, I am with you. I don't want you or any woman to be treated badly." If you are feeling really bold, you might experiment and see what it's like to say, "Yes, you are right. Women have been discriminated against in that way by men. I want you to you to know I'm not aligned with those kinds of values. I'm a man who respects and values a woman's right to full self-expression."

Play with Traditional Roles

One of the best ways to get free of being trapped in any kind of stereotyping, whether traditional or reactionary, is to play with them and have fun. So once a month, or even once a week, or as often as you like, have a date with your partner 1950s style. Just for an evening, go back in time together. Tell her to wear a nice dress and to be ready at 6 p.m. Then have the car waiting outside and some flowers. Remember to open the car door for her when she steps in. Take her to a restaurant that you know she will enjoy, and take the lead in making all the decisions. Remember to take her coat for her and then to help her back on with her coat at the end of the dinner. Pull out the chair for her to sit down. And then, of course, pay the bill. You might like to plan some other little surprises as part of your date as you experiment with taking charge and being the leader and give her the opportunity, just for the evening, to be receptive and follow your lead. Of course, in order for this date to be a total success, you need to gather plenty of information about what would she will like and what will make her happy. You can both take this playfully and see it as a game.

Play with Role Reversal

Similarly, you can get more insight into history together by fully reversing the traditional roles between men and women. This is usually easier if you assume completely fictitious personalities. For example, you might become Philippe from Paris or Cecil from London, who is very sensitive, aesthetic, and shy. Your partner might become Helga from Hamburg, who is tough, muscular, and has a no-nonsense attitude. For a limited period of time, invite her to make all the decisions or to "wear the pants in the house," and allow yourself to become submissive. Perhaps you just need to do this one time so that you can consciously and deliberately react together to stereotyping and playfully experience a full-on total rebellion. Do not take this seriously; to be helpful, it must be fun for everyone.

Reverse Genders

Likewise, perhaps just for five or ten minutes, you and your partner could show each other different aspects of the opposite gender. For five minutes, you could become your idea of what it is like to be a woman. Invite her for a few minutes to assume the role of what she assumes it is like to be a man. Then you could also ask her to show you the guy she really does not want you to be, and you could show her the same for the feminine. For five minutes become your idea of an ideal woman. You can do this in the bedroom as well.

These are all games that you can have fun with. Playing in this way gives you a little distance from the limitations of taking our history too seriously and feeling entrapped within it. Whenever you take any aspect of our identity, play with it, and turn it into art, you are no longer trapped by it. What remains is a free and natural and spontaneous expression of the very best of you.

FOR WOMEN

We celebrate your freedom. Men did not give it to you as it was not theirs to give. But in the last hundred years, women have claimed more and more their right to fully express themselves. Through women, the feminine energy has passed through renaissance after renaissance in the last decades. Every phase of it has been good for women, has been good for humanity, has been good for the planet, and has been good for men too. Men are also evolving. We are shaking off unnecessary constraints on what a man should and should not do and exploring parts of ourselves that were, more or less, completely unavailable to our ancestors.

We all carry resentments and wounds from the past. Every man and every woman has had things happen to them that were painful and that were caused by the opposite gender. We also all can access the pain and restriction of previous generations. A Conscious Man is committed to being awake and alive to every part of himself, to giving the best that he has to give, and to letting go of what no longer works. Meanwhile, a Conscious Woman can recognize that both men and women have operated in the past within narrow restrictions, and both men and women have — in the last decades — experimented with stepping out of the box. And, finally, a Conscious Woman knows how to give the best of herself and how to bring out the best in a man.

A **CONSCIOUS MAN:**

MEET JED DIAMOND, AUTHOR OF *MEN ALIVE*

My wife was a very ardent feminist when we got married in 1966. I saw the women's liberation movement as liberating me, too, because if we liberated women from their restrictive roles and allowed them to be out in the world and enjoy their sexuality, it could be good for me. If women could enjoy their sexuality more, we can have a better time. And if they were out, making a living in the world, it would take pressure off me. I embraced all that. I was right on board with believing that liberation benefited all of us.

There were also views of masculinity that were constraining for me, like the pressure to work in a profession that would lead to financial success—as though I wouldn't be viewed as a real man by the woman in my life if I was doing work I was passionate about, but didn't pay well. My mother came from an era where real men got real jobs and made a living; although she supported my father's creativity, I don't think she respected him. So for me, liberation meant I could work at a job that I really had passion for, regardless of the salary, and that the woman in my life would not only support me, but would be proud of me for doing that kind of work.

Another part of my liberation journey in conscious masculinity came when my wife and I got pregnant. She wanted a natural birth—that was part of the women's movement, too. We studied the Lamaze childbirth technique, and planned on breathing and being together throughout the whole process. But when it came time for the actual birth, we went to a Kaiser Hospital in the East Bay and I was told I would not be able to be in the delivery room. When they wheeled her into the delivery room, they said, "Mr. Diamond, it's time for you to go to the waiting room." I started to walk out, but there was something that wouldn't let me go. I said, "To hell with what the doctor says, this is where I want to be." When I entered the delivery room and held my wife's hand, there was no question of me leaving, no matter what they said. Shortly after my son was born, my wife and I were both crying, and they handed my son to me.

I made a vow to him right then. I even said it out loud: "I commit to being a different kind of father to you than my father was able to be for me. I will commit to doing everything I can to make a different kind of world where men are involved fully in their own lives."

At that time it was a commitment to my son. But from that day in 1969 until today it has been a continuing work—not only for my own son and children and grandchildren, but for everybody's sons and daughters and grandchildren—to create a better world. My calling is to conscious masculinity: to honor my father and his struggles and joys, and to honor those of all other men and women simultaneously.

EPILOGUE

For as long as human beings have been writing things and teaching things, every culture and every generation has had its ideas of what it means to be a man and what it means to be a woman.

Our parents, or maybe grandparents, grew up at the end of an era which restricted men to be cut off from their feelings, to be harsh, and to endure hardships to prove their masculinity. Women were also restricted in a different way.

The last 40 years have seen a dramatic rebellion and reinvention of masculinity and femininity, but it has also seen the enforcement of new and different subtle prisons which can keep us equally restricted.

A Conscious Man is aware of the limited conditioning of his past, as well as his possible reactions to that conditioning, and in that awareness he is set free to find and express his unique self and his unique gifts.

The willingness to question stereotypes, both traditional and counter-traditional allows for your unique flavor to waft into the world, and gives you the opportunity to live the life, and to express the gifts, you were born for.

A Conscious Man is aware of the pressures imposed upon him of what he should do with his life; he is aware of his reaction to and rebellion against those pressures: and so he wakes up to doing the right thing, no matter what.

A Conscious Man feels his duty and calling to fully participate in every aspect of his life, and he also recognizes and respects his need to connect with his innermost wisdom and stillness: and so he brings forth gifts into the world that come from a source beyond his personal, limited mind.

A Conscious Man is aware of the momentum of thousands of years which have defined a man as stoic and unfeeling, but at the same time he is aware of the ways that being taken over by feeling can cause him to become lost and confused: and so he finds the courage to meet the world with an open heart, and to love deeply.

A Conscious Man can feel his instinct to form strong and even dogmatic opinions, and at the same time he is aware of the danger of losing himself to excesses of empathy: and so he learns how to hold a strong and stable space for others to feel safe to speak freely in his company.

A Conscious Man is aware of the habits of his ancestors to bear pain silently, and at the same time he recognizes that in becoming over-emotional he loses both his direction and his humor: and so he learns to feel deeply but not to allow his feelings to escalate into action.

A Conscious Man is aware of the pain and damage caused when anger runs out of control, while at the same time he recognizes that by stuffing his anger into the basement he loses connection with his power: and so he learns to transform his anger into trustworthy and powerful leadership, and becomes a beacon of sanity for all around him.

A Conscious Man knows his tendency to isolate himself or to go into competition with other men. He recognizing his need for connection with other men that offer him structure and challenge: and so he forms deep and lasting friendships that bring out the best in everyone.

A Conscious Man sees the foolishness in pushing through to achieve goals even when circumstances have changed. He also knows that his word needs to mean something real to himself and those close to him: and so he learns to develop deep trust in his capacity to do what he said he would do.

A Conscious Man recognizes that making jokes can be his way to mask insecurity or pain, or even to humiliate others, while at the same time he never loses his recognition of life as play: and so he brings a twinkle to the eyes and a smile to the lips of those whose hearts he touches.

A Conscious Man knows that when lust takes him over it can become greedy and ignorant of boundaries. He also feels the passion in his body that wants to give itself fully: and so he enters into sex as a loving and assertive declaration of pure "yes."

A Conscious Man is aware of the ways that women have sometimes been denigrated and looked down on in the past. He also maintains his dignity and respect for his own masculine essence: and so he develops a deep respect and appreciation for the gifts of the feminine.

A Conscious Man delights in the experience of this very moment, and is reborn now, and now, and now. He is also cognizant that we carry with us centuries of automated responses: and so he learns sensitivity to himself and to everyone around him.

Our hope for you, whoever you may be, is that you may have the opportunity to live a life unencumbered by any kind of "should" or "shouldn't" about what kind of man (or indeed woman) you need to be.

If you got some new ideas from this book and some new ways to experiment with your masculinity, then take a moment now to digest them, to swallow them, and to make them your own so that as you close the book you can feel that you did not get those new ideas from us—they were simply rekindled from out of your own interiority.

If there are things that you did not like in this book, things that did not fit for you, then take a moment now to take a deep inhale and a deep exhale, and let go of those things knowing you never need to think of them again.

We hope that this book has contributed to your freedom more than any idea of conforming to someone else's ideas for you.

We hope that this book has supported you to question your answers as much as it has answered your questions.

John Gray
Arjuna Ardagh

Made in the USA
Las Vegas, NV
31 October 2020